Blue & Gray Magazine's
HISTORY AND TOUR GUIDE
OF THE
ANTIETAM
BATTLEFIELD

FIRST EDITION

COVER: The Dunker Church. Photo by Dave Roth of Blue & Gray Magazine.

ISBN 0-9626034-5-7

Library of Congress Catalog Card Number:

95-76686

TABLE OF CONTENTS

PHOTOGRAPHS

MAPS

BATTLE MAPS

Antietam Battlefield, Sept. 17, 1862

TOUR MAPS

MAP SYMBOLS

⊠	Infantry	I I I	Regiment
⊿	Cavalry	X	Brigade
		X X	Division
▪	Artillery	X X X	Corps
		X X X X	Army
⌐ ¬	Exhausted		
⌊ ⌋		▸	
		⊓	Headquarters

FOREWORD

In 1983 a minor revolution occurred in the Civil War publishing world with the advent of *Blue & Gray Magazine*. The concept was so basic it is amazing that no one had come up with it before: A Civil War magazine that not only discussed the battles, but took the reader there as well. And these were not just standard battlefield tours.

Over the years *Blue & Gray's* faithful readers have journeyed beyond the usual parameters mapped out by Federal and State park agencies to find, as Paul Harvey says, "the rest of the story." The magazine enables readers to visit Civil War sites—long forgotten earthworks and water crossings, historical homes and farms, etc.—sometimes far off the beaten path of major highways and cities.

Two of the most popular issues of *Blue & Gray* covered the Battle of Antietam, published in 1985. Historical commentary in Part I, written by one of the foremost scholars of the battle, the late James Murfin, covered the battle in a concise and interesting fashion that only Jim could do.

Part II included commentary by Murfin and popular author Stephen Sears. It covered sites related to events that occurred in the Sharpsburg, Maryland, area during the battle. This issue allowed readers to see the numerous sites connected with the Battle of Antietam that are outside National Park Service boundaries. Now long out of print, this issue is considered a valuable collector's item.

Blue & Gray editor and publisher Dave Roth has done an excellent job as author of the section known as "The General's Tour." His Antietam tours have stood the test of time and to date rank among the best in the entire *Blue & Gray* series.

With the increased popularity of the Civil War, many new books have come out on the subject. Once in a while someone attempts to write a battlefield guidebook. Sadly, many of these tend to be rather cursory products written by someone that has never seen the battle sites they write about. Much of the material therein is gleaned from a park brochure or a local tourism agency brochure. I know this because over the years I have been contacted by authors and publishers doing these so-called "guidebooks."

Such is not the case with this volume. Indeed, I think it is fair to say that this work and the others in the series will stand as the definitive guidebooks on their respective topics. Or to borrow the idiom from a more recent war— "this is the mother of all Civil War battlefield guides."

Ted Alexander
Historian
Antietam National
Battlefield Park

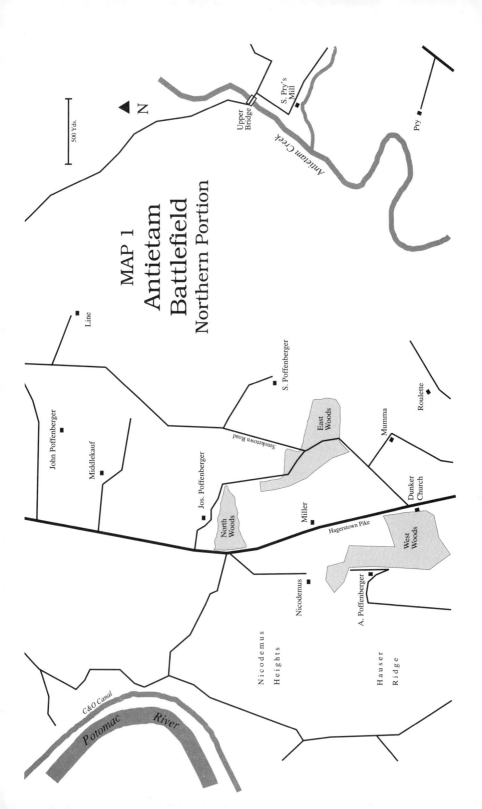

MAP 1
Antietam
Battlefield
Northern Portion

N

500 Yds.

Potomac River

C&O Canal

Nicodemus Heights

Hauser Ridge

John Poffenberger

Middlekauf

Line

Jos. Poffenberger

Smoketown Road

S. Poffenberger

North Woods

East Woods

Miller

Nicodemus

Hagerstown Pike

A. Poffenberger

West Woods

Dunker Church

Mumma

Roulette

Upper Bridge

S. Pry's Mill

Antietam Creek

Pry

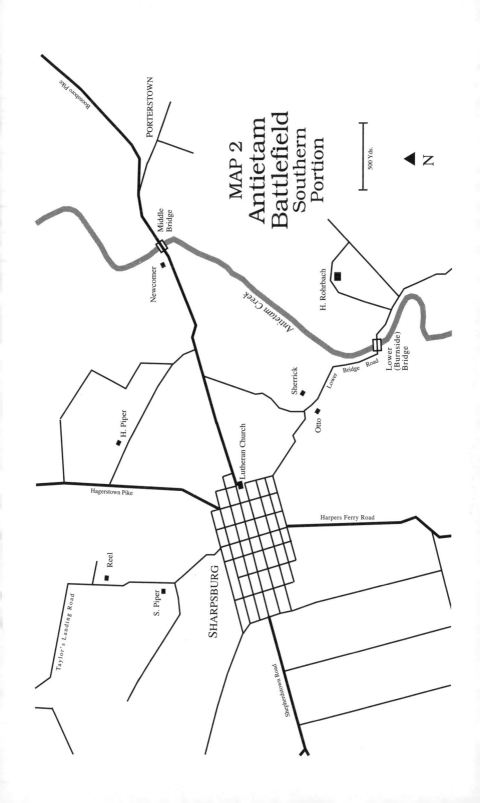

MAP 2
Antietam
Battlefield
Southern
Portion

N

500 Yds.

Boonsboro Pike

PORTERSTOWN

Middle Bridge

Newcomer

Antietam Creek

H. Rohrbach

Lower (Burnside) Bridge

Lower Bridge Road

Sherrick

Otto

H. Piper

Lutheran Church

Hagerstown Pike

Harpers Ferry Road

Reel

S. Piper

SHARPSBURG

Taylor's Landing Road

Shepherdstown Road

Along Antietam Creek
September 17, 1862
Part I

The Introduction to Part I, written by the late James V. Murfin, author of the award-winning THE GLEAM OF BAYONETS (1965) about the Battle of Antietam, focuses broadly on the battle's place in the history of the Civil War: the political climate, high command decisions, and overall strategy. Part I encompasses the sites within the immediate boundaries of the Antietam National Battlefield Park.

Part II of the Antietam tour focuses on sites outside the park boundaries, the out-of-the-way, seldom visited places that are nevertheless significant to a better understanding of the battle, and a more fulfilling visit to the field of fight. Part II begins on Pg. 90.

Introduction

by James V. Murfin

LATE IN SEPTEMBER 1862, a Wisconsin officer wrote his brother from the village of Sharpsburg, Maryland: "We were in the fearful battle at this place on the 17th—it was a great, enormous battle—a great tumbling together of all heaven and earth—the slaughter on both sides was enormous."

Indeed it was. Wednesday, September 17, 1862, ranks as the bloodiest single day of an incomparably bloody civil war. In and around Sharpsburg, along the banks of a sluggish stream known as Antietam Creek, more than 24,000 Americans fell dead or wounded in the course of less than twenty-four hours. It was war at its worst—bruising, vicious, open combat, devoid of much command leadership. Ralph Waldo Emerson might well have had the participants of this engagement in mind when he wrote: "A hero is no braver than an ordinary man, but he is brave five minutes longer."

ON SEPTEMBER 3, 1862, General Robert E. Lee wrote President Jefferson Davis: "The present seems to be the most propitious time since the commencement of the war for the Confederate Army to enter Maryland." By all counts, Lee knew exactly what he was doing, and it was indeed the right time.

Although the war for the Confederacy had thus far been defensive, it had been victorious, and all three of the major campaigns in the East had taken place in Virginia. Two generals in blue had been soundly beaten, and at that moment a third was racing back to the cover of Washington from Bull Run with his tail between his legs. It was clearly time for a reappraisal of Confederate strategy. Lee was not long in making up his mind.

Aside from the need of subsistence, always a basic and compelling reason, Lee had six motives for invading the North. First, "The purpose, if discovered," Lee wrote, "will have the effect of carrying the [war] north of the Potomac." Lee knew he would be discovered and he was well aware of the psychological effect an invasion would have on Washington and the North. Up to this point in history, psychological warfare, as we know it today, was virtually unknown. Although nowhere in Lee's papers does such a theme run, the invasion of Maryland was a brilliantly calculated move to unnerve the Federal government in a time of crisis.

Secondly, "If it is ever desired to give material aid to Maryland," Lee continued, "and afford her an opportunity of throwing off the oppression to which she is now subject, this would seem the most favorable." Maryland was a border state in the truest sense. The eastern shore and southern counties, which surrounded Washington, were almost entirely agricultural, maintaining a close relationship with Virginia through their traditional colonial ties as well as their large annual tobacco crop.

Slavery was still an established institution there and the people openly exhibited Southern sympathies. Lee

Robert E. Lee

James Longstreet

Stonewall Jackson

labored under the false impression that the central and western counties, which he had decided to invade, shared these same sentiments. Contrary to his belief, he would be entering a section of the state which, economically and socially, was on the same level as the North.

Agriculture had also played an important role in the development of these counties, but old colonial traditions were rapidly being pushed aside for industry, better roads, and other social improvements. Slavery had been discarded in favor of skilled labor. They were far from being void of Southern sentiments, however; hundreds of families were divided, and among these Lee would find a few friends.

Thirdly, "We can not afford to be idle," Lee wrote, "and though weaker than our opponents in men and military equipment, [we] must endeavor to harass, if we can not destroy them. I am aware that the moment is attended with much risk, yet I do not consider success impossible, and shall endeavor to guard it from loss. As long as the army of the enemy are employed on this frontier, I have no fears for the safety of Richmond. . . ." Although Confederate intelligence had proved superior in many ways to the Federal army's, Lee could only guess what move the Union might next make. Should it be an offensive one, it would surely be aimed at Richmond. If Lee invaded now, the Union army would have to follow and would do so with all its concentrated forces, thus forestalling further pressure on the Confederate capital.

Fourthly, "Should the results of the expedition justify it," Lee told Davis, "I propose to enter Pennsylvania. . . ." As the Mississippi River was to the Confederacy, the

Baltimore & Ohio and Pennsylvania railroads were to the Union. They were not only main lines of supply to the West, but vital lines of communications. The B&O, although running on the border, as it were, was solidly controlled by strong Union support. Once Lee crossed the Potomac, B&O traffic would be interrupted. Then, if he were in a strong defensive position, his next target would be the Pennsylvania Railroad. He intended to march on Harrisburg where he would destroy the Susquehanna River bridge. Once this was accomplished, and only then, would he consider moves on Baltimore and Washington.

Lee's next reason for invasion was of primary importance to the cause for Southern independence. Both England and France were favorably impressed with the Confederacy's progress in the war. Although they had not recognized it as an independent nation, they had given it belligerent rights, which meant, in essence, ceasing to regard Confederate ships as mere pirates on the open seas. Cotton was extremely important to both nations, a point of diplomatic negotiations which the Confederate government had not failed to exploit. Also, the ineffectiveness, at that time, of Lincoln's naval blockade of the South was proving an important advantage for negotiations. The time was ripe for recognition.

If England recognized the Confederacy, France was certain to follow suit. This move would then accomplish one of two things: either bring an immediate stop to hostilities or push the United States dangerously close to international crisis and perhaps global war. In either case, the Richmond government was sure to gain. The Confederate States of America could become a sovereign and independent nation.

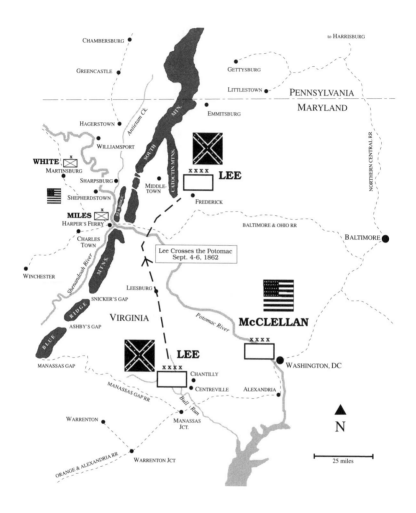

MAP 3

Maryland Campaign

Situation on Sept. 7, 1862

The string of Confederate victories to date had almost convinced England that recognition was feasible. Early in September, while Lincoln fretted over the defenses of Washington, British Prime Minister, the Viscount Palmerston, and Lord John Russell, British Foreign Minister, agreed to call a cabinet meeting in early October for the purpose of discussing the Confederacy. Europe's eyes were on Lee's progress and Lee knew what was at stake.

The sixth reason for this invasion of enemy territory was Lee's hope to influence the forthcoming Northern Congressional elections. In the election of 1860, the Republican Party had come to power on two main factors: the split in the Democratic Party, which had been transpiring during the Buchanan administration, and the platform on the slavery-freedom issue. To some, then, the answer to the South's problems did not lie in secession, rather, in the acquisition of Northern allies in Congress and in the courts. Lee figured that the needed influence could be bought, not by money and political skulduggery, but by a military victory on Northern soil. If it could be accomplished before election time in the fall, pressure could be brought to bear in the right political circles; a reunited Democratic Party would hold the balance of power, and before another spring had set in, the United States would be ready to negotiate with the Confederate States.

In short, Lee's strategy was to harass the Army of the Potomac by feigning an attack on Washington, thus drawing away any threats to Richmond. At the same time, he would seek the support of Maryland. If all went well, he would advance to Pennsylvania, secure a "beach-head" north of the Mason-Dixon line, and most assuredly bring on foreign intervention in one form or another. In any event, the fall election in the North would bring drastic changes advantageous to the Southern cause. Lee developed what today would be called a "wait and see" policy. Though he had certain goals and accomplishments to attain, he would plan his campaign as he marched, basing it on the often unpredictable actions of the enemy and its general.

There are few points in world history when a nation— if that term can be used—had so much at stake, so much riding on an army of 70,000 men, at full strength, perhaps 50,000 by the time they crossed the Potomac, and, at best, 35,000 by the time of battle.

WHILE LEE WAS MAKING HIS PLANS , the powers-that-be in Washington were not sitting idly by. George Brinton McClellan, 36-year-old major general, who had seen the church spires of Richmond only a few months before, but had failed to take the city, was called back to command of the Army of the Potomac by President Lincoln. Despite his failures on the battlefield, McClellan was considered by Lincoln to be the only man who could reorganize a defeated army. And he did perform miracles. Within days, while Lee marched toward the Potomac, McClellan had his massive army ready, and on the day Lee crossed the river at White's Ford, near Leesburg, Virginia, McClellan moved from Washington into the Maryland countryside.

Then Lee did a curious thing that has given pause to historians for more than a century. At Frederick, he made a decision, a bold and daring decision for which he has been called the "master of the calculated risk." With full knowledge that McClellan was pursuing him, Lee split his outnumbered army into five parts, three to surround and take the Federal garrison of 13,000 men at Harper's Ferry, one to Hagerstown to guard against any Federal move from Pennsylvania, and one to be stationed on the old National Pike at South Mountain near Boonsboro. To inform his staff of the plan, Lee had written Special Orders No. 191, and copies were sent out by courier to his principal general officers. Without further delay, the Army of Northern Virginia moved on.

As the various Federal regiments arrived in Frederick in their pursuit of Lee, they pitched their tents in the same fields as had the Confederates. At about noon on September 13, the 27th Indiana arrived. The arms were stacked, regimental flags furled, and the brisk business of establishing normal camp operations were set into motion. Those without specific duties wandered off to rest from the morning's pace.

Corporal Barton W. Mitchell and Sergeant John M. Bloss tossed their gear aside and lay down on the cool grass. They lapsed into the idle talk of soldiers, discussing McClellan's return as their leader, or perhaps a recent letter from home. Mitchell had just rolled over and was about to pull his cap over his eyes when he spotted a piece of paper wrapped around what appeared to be several sticks. Upon investigation, he found it to be three cigars of some expense.

This type of luxury was not easy to come by for the common soldier. While they leaned back like men of leisure and prepared to light up, they opened the paper and made a quick survey. Suddenly the cigars became insignificant. The paper they held in their hands was of

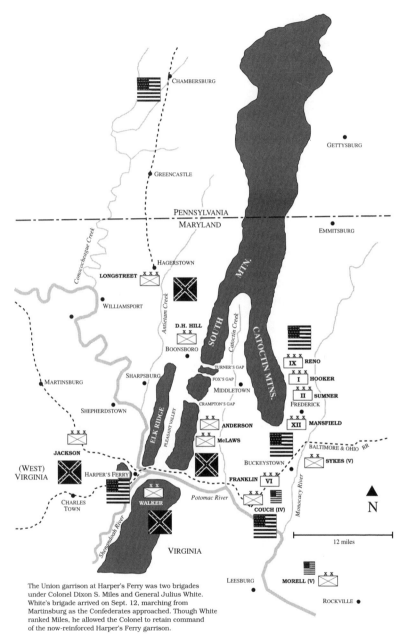

CHAMBERSBURG

GETTYSBURG

GREENCASTLE

PENNSYLVANIA
MARYLAND

EMMITSBURG

Conococheague Creek

HAGERSTOWN

LONGSTREET

WILLIAMSPORT

Antietam Creek

SOUTH MTN.

Catoctin Creek

CATOCTIN MTNS.

D.H. HILL

BOONSBORO

IX RENO

I HOOKER

TURNER'S GAP

FOX'S GAP

MIDDLETOWN

II SUMNER

FREDERICK

MARTINSBURG

SHARPSBURG

CRAMPTON'S GAP

XII MANSFIELD

SHEPHERDSTOWN

ELK RIDGE

PLEASANT VALLEY

ANDERSON

McLAWS

JACKSON

BALTIMORE & OHIO RR

BUCKEYSTOWN

SYKES (V)

(WEST)
VIRGINIA

HARPER'S FERRY

FRANKLIN VI

CHARLES
TOWN

WALKER

Potomac River

COUCH (IV)

Monocacy River

12 miles

Shenandoah River

VIRGINIA

LEESBURG

MORELL (V)

ROCKVILLE

N

The Union garrison at Harper's Ferry was two brigades
under Colonel Dixon S. Miles and General Julius White.
White's brigade arrived on Sept. 12, marching from
Martinsburg as the Confederates approached. Though White
ranked Miles, he allowed the Colonel to retain command
of the now-reinforced Harper's Ferry garrison.

MAP 4
Maryland Campaign
Situation on Sept. 13, 1862

obvious vital military importance. Bloss read the names of
Jackson, Longstreet, and Lee, names he knew well. At
once the two men delivered their find to Colonel Silas
Colgrove, their commander. Colgrove immediately saw
that he held in his hands the key to the Confederate
operations. It read: "Headquarters, Army of Northern
Virginia, Special Orders No. 191." The paper was signed:
"By command of General R. E. Lee: R. H. Chilton, Assistant Adjutant-General."

In a matter of minutes Colgrove met with Colonel S.
E. Pittman, division adjutant and, by chance, an old
friend of Robert Chilton's. Pittman quickly identified
Chilton's signature and rushed to report to General
McClellan. McClellan was overjoyed. The game was over.
He now knew Lee's secret, he exclaimed. A few moments
later, while talking to his close friend General John
Gibbon, McClellan said, "Here is a paper with which, if I
cannot whip Bobbie Lee, I will be willing to go home."

General Lee was now in a difficult position, but he was
spared by McClellan's inability to do what he had declared
he would do: move immediately. Debate continues today as
to why McClellan did not speed his army to South Mountain
and Harper's Ferry and swallow in one vast gulp the
separate wings of Lee's army. As it was, by the time the
Union Army made its way to South Mountain on Sunday,
September 14, Lee had regrouped two of his five divisions
and held position long enough to alter his course of action
and determine to stand and fight along Antietam Creek.

The Confederates suffered staggering losses in the
fighting at South Mountain and for the first time since
they had crossed the river, the future looked bleak. Hope

of going on to Pennsylvania faded. Virtually no encouragement or support had come from the people of Maryland; sources of food and supplies were little better than in Virginia; and with three divisions of the army still at Harper's Ferry, hopes of fighting McClellan in Maryland at all seemed to dwindle. A stand at Sharpsburg, at best, would avoid total destruction.

Daylight was slow in coming on the morning of Wednesday, September 17, 1862. Rain the night before had left a heavy mist that covered the fields. But as the first faint streaks of sunlight appeared over the mountain, the artillery began to roar. Battle had begun. Lee's Army of Northern Virginia—35,000 determined men who had been marching and fighting steadily for nearly six months, who were several hundred miles from home, many without shoes and adequate clothing, and even less with proper food—defiantly squared off against the mightiest army ever assembled on the North American continent. McClellan had some 87,000 troops, with the finest equipment, the best supplies, thousands of fresh troops in reserve, and the most sophisticated organization, who were on home territory with lines of communication unequaled anywhere.

These were the odds—more than two to one. By all rights, at the end of the day, Lee's small army should have been crushed. This was what Lincoln wanted. This was what he asked of his general. This was what he almost got.

ABOUT THE AUTHOR: The late JAMES V. MURFIN grew up near the Antietam battlefield and later turned his fascination with the place into the first major work on the battle, *The Gleam of Bayonets*.

Antietam Battle Maps

September 17, 1862

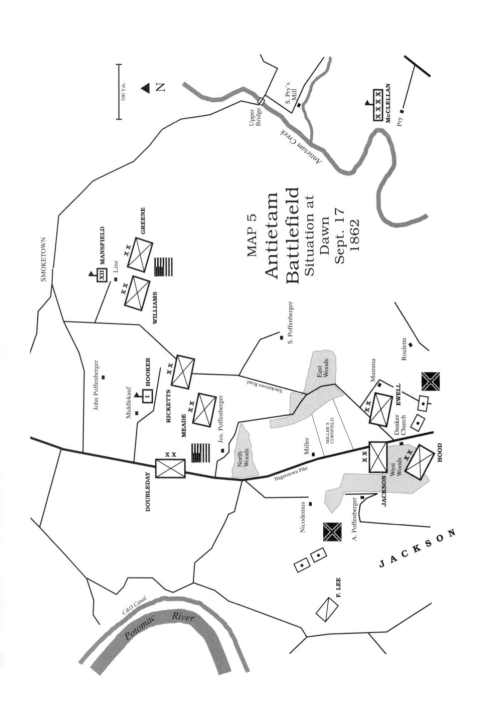

MAP 5
Antietam
Battlefield
Situation at
Dawn
Sept. 17
1862

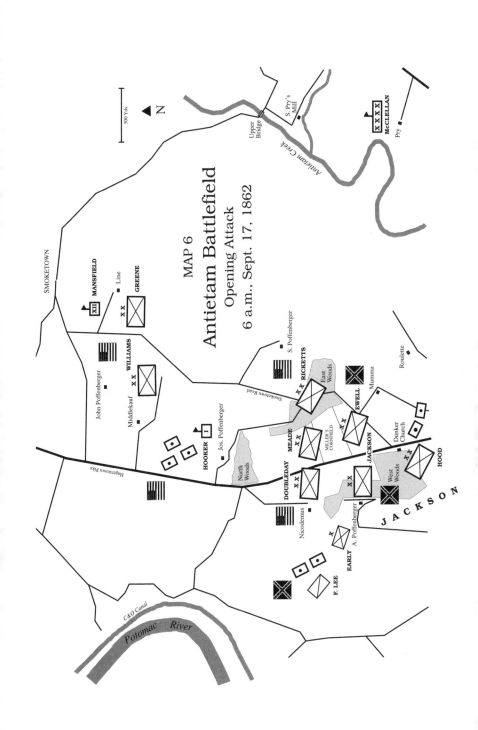

MAP 6
Antietam Battlefield
Opening Attack
6 a.m., Sept. 17, 1862

N   500 Yds.

Potomac River

C&O Canal

SMOKETOWN

Hagerstown Pike

John Poffenberger

Middlekauf

WILLIAMS
XX

MANSFIELD
XII   Line

GREENE
XX

S. Poffenberger

Jos. Poffenberger

North Woods

HOOKER
I

DOUBLEDAY
XX

Nicodemus

F. LEE

EARLY
X

A. Poffenberger

JACKSON

West Woods

JACKSON
XX

MEADE
XX

MILLER'S CORNFIELD

RICKETTS
XX

Smoketown Road

East Woods

EWELL
XX

Mumma

Dunker Church

HOOD
XX

Roulette

Upper Bridge

S. Pry's Mill

Antietam Creek

McCLELLAN
XXXX

Pry

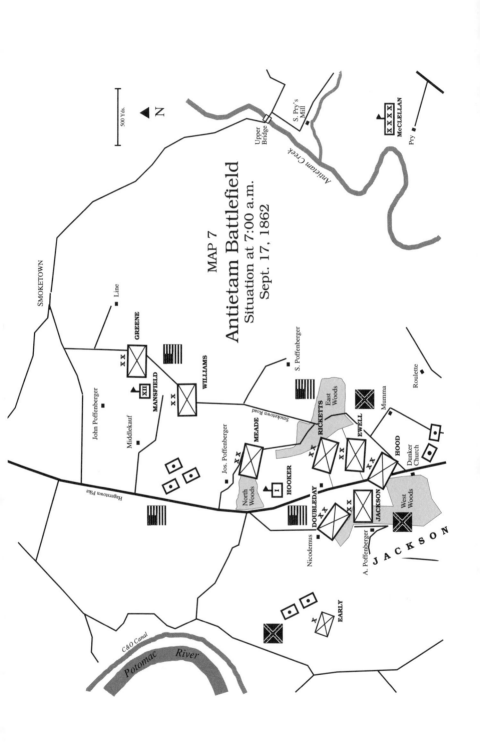

MAP 7
Antietam Battlefield
Situation at 7:00 a.m.
Sept. 17, 1862

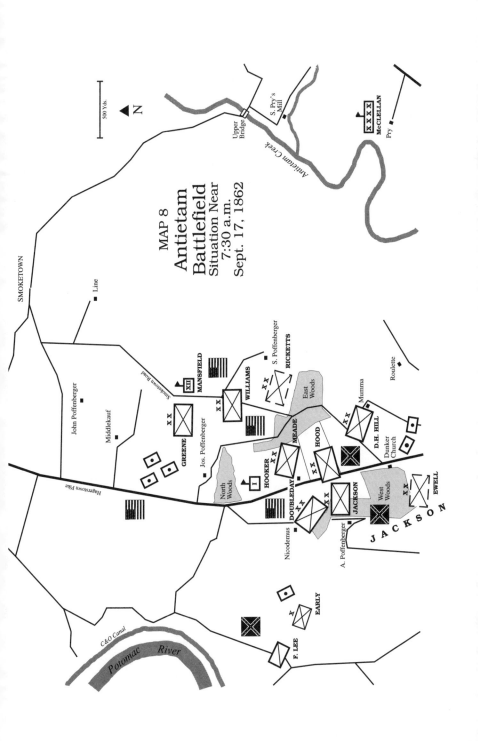

MAP 8
Antietam
Battlefield
Situation Near
7:30 a.m.
Sept. 17, 1862

500 Yds.

N

SMOKETOWN

Line

John Poffenberger

Middlekauf

Smoketown Road

MANSFIELD
XII

GREENE
XX

Jos. Poffenberger

WILLIAMS
XX

XX

WILLIAMS

S. Poffenberger

RICKETTS

East
Woods

MEADE
XX

HOOD
XX

D.H. HILL
XX

Mumma

Roulette

Dunker
Church

Hagerstown Pike

North
Woods

HOOKER
I

DOUBLEDAY
XX

JACKSON
XX

West
Woods

JACKSON

EWELL
XX

Nicodemus

A. Poffenberger

J A C K S O N

C&O Canal

Potomac   River

F. LEE

EARLY

Upper
Bridge

S. Pry's
Mill

Antietam Creek

McCLELLAN
XXXX

Pry

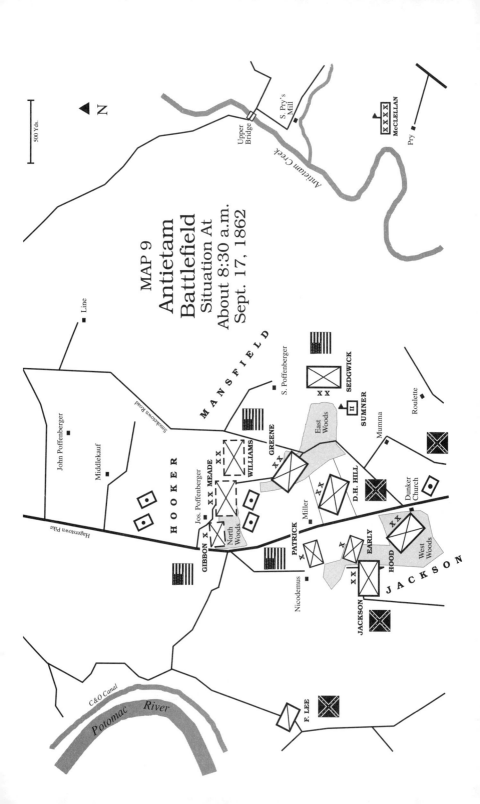

MAP 9
Antietam
Battlefield
Situation At
About 8:30 a.m.
Sept. 17, 1862

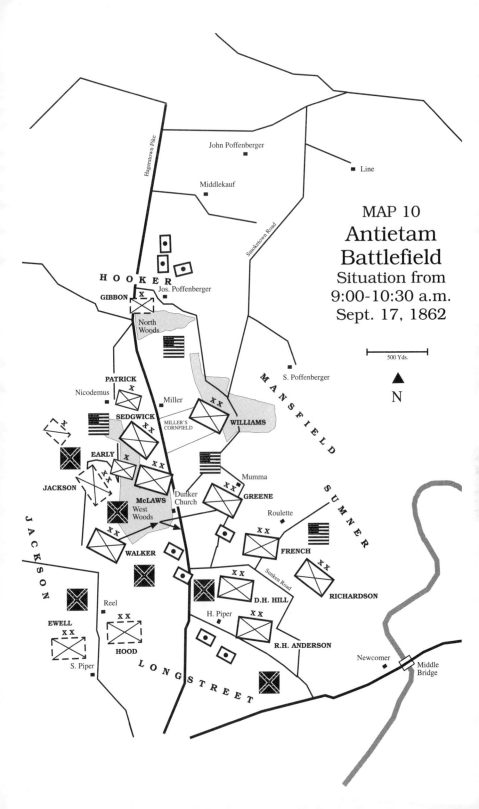

MAP 10
**Antietam
Battlefield**
Situation from
9:00-10:30 a.m.
Sept. 17, 1862

500 Yds.

N

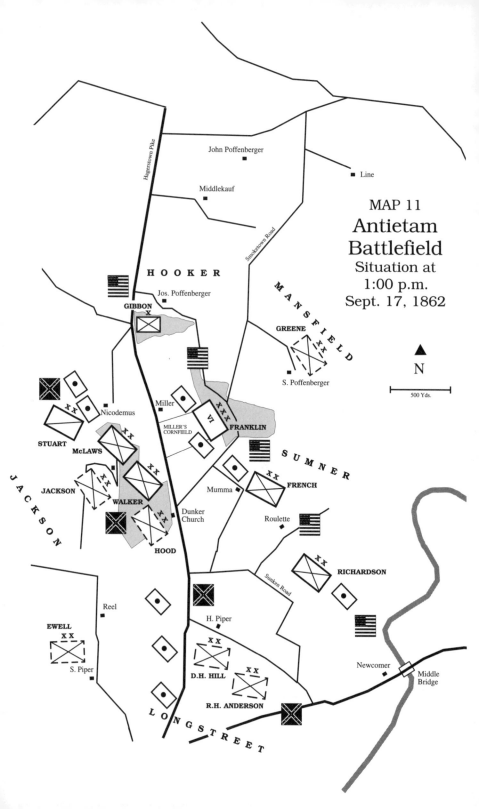

MAP 11
**Antietam
Battlefield**
Situation at
1:00 p.m.
Sept. 17, 1862

N

500 Yds.

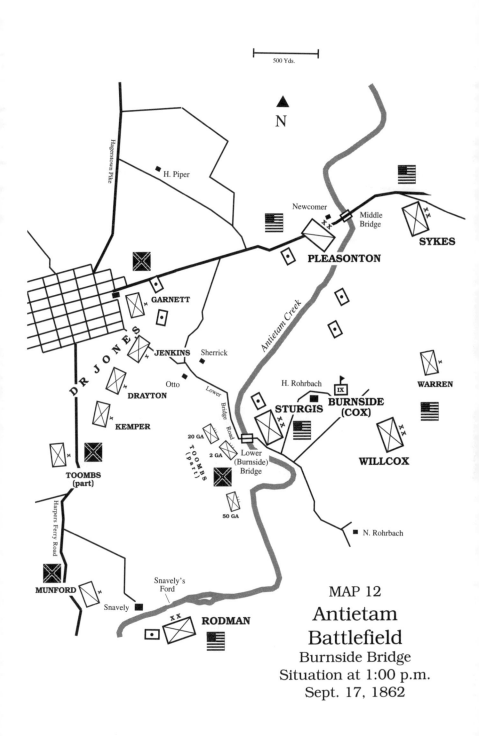

500 Yds.

N

H. Piper

Newcomer

Middle
Bridge

SYKES

PLEASONTON

GARNETT

Antietam Creek

DR JONES

JENKINS   Sherrick

WARREN

DRAYTON   Otto

H. Rohrbach

IX

KEMPER

STURGIS   BURNSIDE
(COX)

20 GA

WILLCOX

2 GA   Lower
(Burnside)
Bridge

TOOMBS
(part)

50 GA

N. Rohrbach

TOOMBS
(part)

MUNFORD

Snavely's
Ford

Snavely

MAP 12
Antietam
Battlefield
Burnside Bridge
Situation at 1:00 p.m.
Sept. 17, 1862

RODMAN

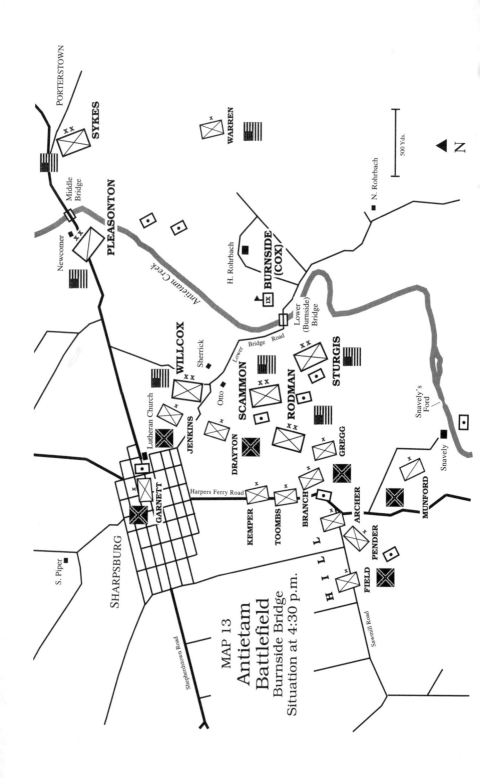

MAP 13
Antietam
Battlefield
Burnside Bridge
Situation at 4:30 p.m.

The Battle of
Antietam

by the Editors of Blue & Gray Magazine

AFTER THE BATTLE OF Second Manassas (Bull Run), fought August 29-30, 1862, in which the Union army under Major General John Pope, styled the Army of Virginia, was soundly defeated by Lee's Army of Northern Virginia on old familiar terrain in the very backyard of the national capital, the Confederates decided the time was right for their first invasion of the North. Accordingly, on September 3, Lee started his march for the Potomac River and on the 4th began crossing at White's Ford near Leesburg, Virginia.

Many Confederates refused to cross the river; they had enlisted to defend their homeland, not to become invaders. Other men were lost to Lee simply because of the change in terrain. The shoeless, who accounted for a large part of Lee's army, could endure marching barefoot on the soft Virginia clay, but the rocky roads and rough terrain of the Maryland countryside forced many out of the line of march. Still others departed the ranks simply because of the season—it was harvest time—with the intentions of returning to the army after the family crops were in. As well, Lee's hope to swell his ranks with "liberated" Marylanders ended in disappointment as the border state's Rebel sentiments were found to be grossly misjudged, at least along the path of Lee's invasion.

The army marched into Frederick, Maryland, on the morning of September 6, and there Lee engineered a grand scheme. The army was divided into four parts: One, under Major General Stonewall Jackson, was to proceed west, then south, then east to converge on the Union garrison of some 13,000 men at Harper's Ferry. This was to be done in concert with the second and third parts. One of those parts was under Major General Lafayette McLaws, composed of his own division plus that of Major General Richard H. Anderson. The other part was under Brigadier General John G. Walker, and consisted of his small two-brigade division. These two parts were to approach Harper's Ferry from the north (Maryland Heights) and south (Loudoun Heights), respectively, to force the garrison's hoped-for quick surrender.

Lee, with the fourth part, Major General James Longstreet's corps (minus Walker's, McLaws' and Anderson's divisions), and Major General D. H. Hill's division of Jackson's corps, along with the bulk of Major General Jeb Stuart's cavalry, were to continue northward to Boonsboro, west of South Mountain and its important passes. Lee's plan, spelled out in Special Orders No. 191, went against the grain of all acceptable precepts of making war. The enigmatic Jackson grinned slyly at the opportunity; the methodical Longstreet cringed mournfully at the prospects.

To make matters worse, one copy of the order was carelessly wrapped around three cigars, was left behind in camp when the Confederates departed Frederick, and found its way into Major General George B. McClellan's hands. Meanwhile, much to Longstreet's chagrin, the army was split into yet a fifth part, as D. H. Hill was left at Boonsboro while Longstreet's two divisions marched to Hagerstown to contend with the rumored threat of a large Federal force advancing south from Pennsylvania.

AFTER SECOND MANASSAS, Pope's defeated Army of Virginia was consolidated into the Army of the Potomac, most of the latter having just arrived after the evacuation of the Peninsula below Richmond. The "new" army was regrouped and rejuvenated under the careful direction of the Union's master organizer, McClellan. Although he never admitted his inglorious showing on the Peninsula, it was, nevertheless, behind him.

Little Mac embarked with enthusiasm in his pursuit of the Confederates, so enthusiastically that Lee could not help but notice a marked change in the usually predictable Federal commander. It is a matter of uncertainty whether Lee knew that his Orders 191 had fallen into McClellan's possession, but it is safe to say that by nightfall of the same day that Corporal Mitchell picked up the wrapped cigars, September 13, Lee was aware that certain intelligence of his movements had been lost or betrayed to the enemy.

McClellan's reorganized Army of the Potomac, which had followed Lee's army to Frederick and arrived on September 13, three days after the Confederates had left the place, consisted of three wings:

LEFT WING—Commanded by Major General William B. Franklin, composed of his VI Corps plus Major General Darius Couch's division of the IV Corps.

CENTER WING—Commanded by Major General Edwin V. Sumner, composed of his II Corps and Major General Joseph K. F. Mansfield's XII Corps.

RIGHT WING—Commanded by Major General Ambrose E. Burnside, composed of the IX Corps under Major General Jesse L. Reno, and Major General Joseph Hooker's I Corps.

The Cavalry Division was commanded by Brigadier General Alfred Pleasonton, and before battle was joined, Major General Fitz John Porter's V Corps would be summoned from the defenses of Washington to reinforce the always undergunned—or so he always thought—McClellan.*

---

* McClellan would abandon his "three-wing" organization before his army met Lee's on Sharpsburg Ridge. He unraveled the system when, apparently, actual tactical movements required handier dispersions of units, leaving at least one of the wing commanders, Burnside, pouting over the partial loss of command authority.

George B. McClellan

Left to right: Fitz John Porter, commander of the V Corps, and Little Mac's chief confidant; Edwin V. Sumner, II Corps; and William B. Franklin, VI Corps.

On the 14th, McClellan moved from Frederick to seize the passes through South Mountain, ready to exploit his new-found advantage of the verified "lost order" by interjecting his men between the scattered elements of Lee's army, in the hope of defeating in detail his off-balance foe. Hooker's corps swung north to attack Turner's Gap. He was supported by Reno's corps, which did most of its fighting a short distance south of Turner's, at Fox's Gap, where Reno was killed in the bloody action there. Franklin was to lead his infantry against another gap, Crampton's, a few miles below Fox's Gap.

At South Mountain, D. H. Hill, reinforced by troops arriving from Longstreet's command, savagely opposed the gathering blue horde that spread across the valley in what Hill called a sight "grand and sublime" in its magnitude, yet he confirmed the wisdom of the Biblical phrase, "as terrible as an army with banners." The attacks came late and Hill's reinforced troops managed to hold on until evening, delaying the Federal advance, but the Confederates were outgunned, so Lee ordered them to fall back on Sharpsburg that night.

McClellan now had the gaps in South Mountain. The least defended of the gaps, Crampton's, was attacked and seized by Franklin, but his assault came too late in the day and darkness prevented further penetration. Thus, valuable time was lost to the Union effort, gaining Lee the precious hours needed for Jackson to take Harper's Ferry. What earlier seemed the demise of Lee's invasion had taken a favorable turn for the Confederates, and soon encouraging news came from Jackson, who predicted that Harper's Ferry "through God's blessing" would fall to him next day.

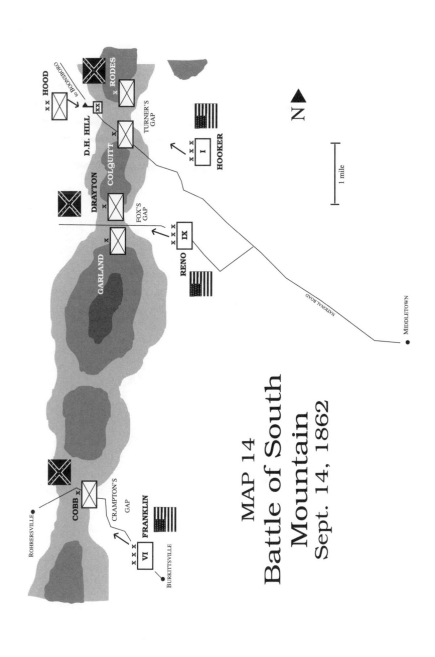

MAP 14
Battle of South
Mountain
Sept. 14, 1862

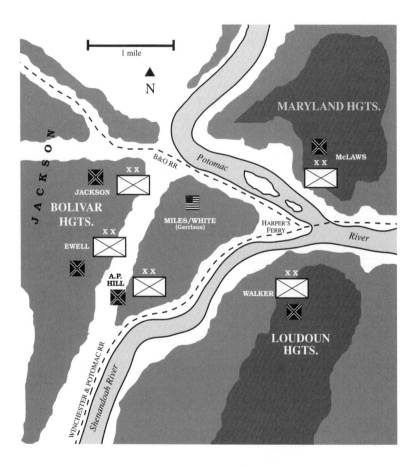

MAP 15

Jackson's Siege of Harper's Ferry
Situation on Sept. 15, 1862

At McClellan's camp, most of the 15th was spent in joyous celebration of their South Mountain victory—tardy as it was. And true enough, Lee was startled at the sudden boldness of his opponent. McClellan had engineered a great coup with his seizure of the mountain passes, but he would fritter away his advantage in typical McClellan style: stalling. The commanding general made no inspection of his prize until the afternoon of the 15th and concluded that it was too late to initiate a follow-up attack.

Meanwhile, Jackson forced the surrender of almost 12,000 Union men at Harper's Ferry and bagged considerable amounts of supplies, 13,000 small arms, and 73 artillery pieces. Thus, McClellan's idling time away permitted most of Jackson's men to begin their march to join Lee, except A. P. Hill's Light Division, left behind to complete the details of surrender. Lee decided to stand and fight on Sharpsburg Ridge with his back to the Potomac.*

IT WAS NOT UNTIL the afternoon of the 16th that McClellan issued orders for his army to move against Lee at Sharpsburg. The two armies were separated by a few miles of gently rolling terrain, among neat German farms, fields of mature grain, and a nuisance of a little, twisting stream, the Antietam. McClellan's vague battle plan seems to have centered on a main attack from the north by Hooker's I Corps, with assistance from Sumner's II and Mansfield's XII corps. A crossing of the Antietam to strike

---

* A bit of drama occurred on the evening prior to the surrender of Harper's Ferry when more than a thousand Union cavalrymen under the Mississippi-born New York colonel, "Grimes" Davis, escaped under cover of darkness.

the Confederate right was to be forced at the Lower (or Rohrbach) Bridge by troops under Ambrose E. Burnside.

Massed at the center of McClellan's line was Porter's V Corps and, in outdated Napoleonic style, the bulk of the army's cavalry, poised to smash through the center of Lee's line at the precise moment to secure a brilliant victory: a classic history-book battle from the days when horsemen were the flower of the army. But weapons technology by the time of the Civil War had changed all that. In contrast, Lee's cavalry anchored both his flanks and, above all, had expertly reconnoitered the future battlefield, determining the crossings of the Antietam, the roads, the nature of the terrain, and the probable avenues of attack.

The Federal commander, perhaps on his mind the predicament he had placed Lee by capturing his Special Orders No. 191, issued no general orders for the battle. He also thought Lee outnumbered him by great odds, estimating the enemy's numbers at 100,000, when in truth the Confederates mustered only about 35,000 men of all arms to face the Union's 87,000. (Some accounts put the number of McClellan's "effectives" at 70,000.) Laboring under these misconceptions renders more heinous McClellan's neglect in not initiating a proper reconnaissance and failing to coordinate and deliver a clear plan of battle.

Any measure of surprise that might have thrown Lee's defensive plan off balance was lost when on the late afternoon of the 16th Hooker crossed the Antietam at the Upper Bridge and went into camp, followed later that night by Mansfield's corps, stumbling through darkness and a light rain to a point left of and slightly in rear of

Hooker's corps. Mansfield's men could not guide on the I Corps' campfires because McClellan had lately decided to ban fires in a clear-cut act of closing the barn door after the horse had gone.

Skirmish fire erupted near sunset in what came to be called the East Woods. Brigadier General George G. Meade's division in the advance of Hooker's I Corps, screening the column, slammed into Brigadier General John Bell Hood's division, sent by Lee to intercept the Federal movement. Artillery was brought to bear and the fight waxed warm until darkness ended the exchange. Therefore, the first Antietam casualties occurred on the eve of the war's bloodiest day. As Hooker's men bedded down in the damp blackness, Lee, blessed with a glimpse of McClellan's hand, shifted men to his left.

Thus, the stage was set for the bloodiest single day of the Civil War, when 24,000 Americans out of an estimated 125,000 were listed among the killed, wounded, captured or missing.

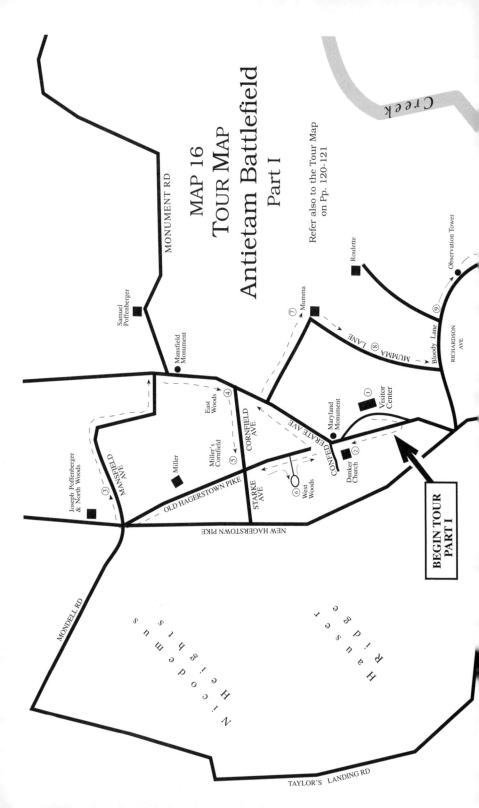

MAP 16
TOUR MAP
Antietam Battlefield
Part I

Refer also to the Tour Map
on Pp. 120-121

Creek

MONUMENT RD

Samuel
Poffenberger

Mansfield Monument

Roulette

Mumma ⑦

MUMMA LANE ⑧

Bloody Lane

Observation Tower

RICHARDSON AVE

Joseph Poffenberger
& North Woods ③

MANSFIELD AVE

East Woods

Miller

Miller's Cornfield

CORNFIELD AVE ④

⑤

CONFEDERATE AVE

Maryland Monument

Visitor Center ①

Dunker Church ②

OLD HAGERSTOWN PIKE

STARKE AVE

West Woods ⑥

NEW HAGERSTOWN PIKE

BEGIN TOUR
PART I

MONDELL RD

Nicodemus Heights

Hauser Ridge

TAYLOR'S LANDING RD

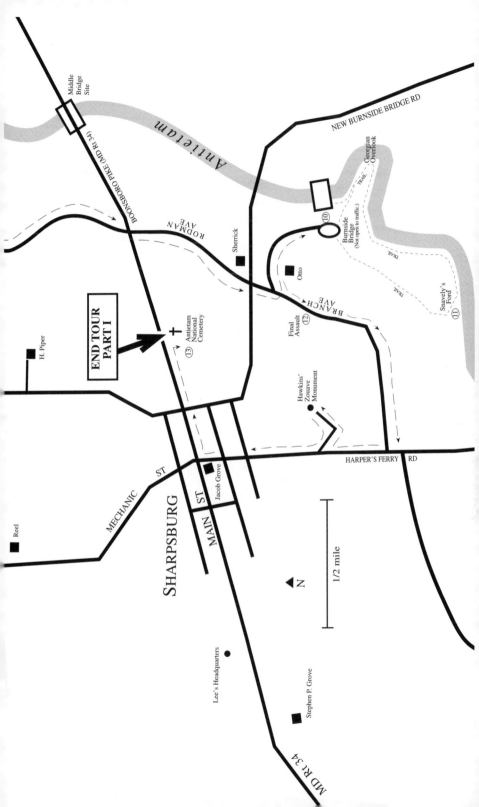

Middle Bridge Site

BOONSBORO PIKE (MD Rt 34)

Antietam

NEW BURNSIDE BRIDGE RD

Georgian Overlook

TRAIL

RODMAN AVE

⑩

Burnside Bridge (Not open to traffic.)

TRAIL

Sherrick

TRAIL

TRAIL

Otto

Snavely's Ford

⑪

END TOUR PART I

Antietam National Cemetery

⑬

BRANCH AVE

Final Assault ⑫

H. Piper

Hawkins' Zouave Monument

Reel

MECHANIC

ST

SHARPSBURG

MAIN ST

Jacob Grove

HARPER'S FERRY RD

N

1/2 mile

Lee's Headquarters

Stephen P. Grove

MD Rt 34

The Battle of Antietam

Driving Tour of Part I Begins Here

Detailed background information, descriptions of troop movements, instances of personal heroism, human interest stories, etc., are included under each Tour Stop heading. The order of appearance of the headings follows the tour route laid out by the National Park Service.

1. ANTIETAM NATIONAL BATTLEFIELD VISITOR CENTER

Begin your Antietam tour at the National Park Service Visitor Center, located off Hagerstown Pike (MD Rt. 65) twelve miles south of Hagerstown, Maryland, and one mile north of the town of Sharpsburg. The Visitor Center has exhibits, a book store, and an interpretive film. Living history demonstrations are a regular part of the park's seasonal interpretation and include, at various times, camp settings, cavalry drills, and cannon-crew firing procedures.

The Visitor Center is well-situated on high ground between the Dunker Church and the Sunken Road (Bloody

Lane), and its observation deck offers a commanding view of the morning and midday phases of the battle. The grounds of the Visitor Center contain impressive artillery displays, interpretative markers, and monuments, in particular, the Maryland Monument, dedicated to her eight regiments that fought at Antietam (Sharpsburg), two Confederate and six Union.*

As if General McClellan had envisioned a future battlefield park at Antietam, and planned for ease of visitation and simplified interpretation for posterity, his attacks can be classified into three distinct phases in a roughly north-to-south geographical flow—a very orderly layout, much what one might expect from the master organizer, though not particularly the optimum battle plan for the decisive victory that could very well have been his.

The "morning phase," 6:00 a.m. to about 9:30 a.m., is Hooker's attack—soon joined by Sumner and Mansfield— against the Confederate left, and includes the fighting in Miller's cornfield, around the Dunker Church and in the West Woods, and the East Woods.

The second, or "midday phase," from 9:30 a.m. to 1:00 p.m., is the attack of Sumner's two divisions against the approximate center of the Confederate line: D. H. Hill's division in the Sunken Road.

---

* With all due respect to the Southern preference of battle names, and to avoid awkward and repetitive dual-naming, the National Park Service's designated title "Antietam Battle-field" or "Battle of Antietam" will be used henceforth in the text, and "Sharpsburg"—the Southern preference for the battle—will be used only in references to the town.

And the third, or "afternoon phase," from about 1:00 p.m. to 5:30 p.m., occurs as Burnside's troops finally force their way across the Antietam at the Lower Bridge and threaten to roll up the Confederate right.

Throughout these various phases and along the various points of attack, Lee was able to shift his forces to meet each new threat, using to the fullest his advantages of concealed interior lines, superior command control, and the intangible but very evident "victory momentum," or winning spirit, that transformed hungry, ragtag soldiers into highly mobile fighting machines. The latter factor can not be dismissed nor should it be underestimated. The phenomenon of "winner's luck" was as evident that day as if it represented an additional corps in Lee's camp. For example, just when it looked as if the battle was lost, the Virginia flag appeared on the horizon to meet Burnside's attack; Lee nodded as if he knew all along that reinforcements would arrive at just the right time.

The Visitor Center sits on ground fought over during both the morning and midday phases. It occupies the site of Confederate colonel Stephen D. Lee's artillery battalion: four batteries (out of six in his battalion) that laid down a murderous fire on Hooker's advance out of the North and East woods into Miller's cornfield. A crossfire from Pelham's guns on Nicodemus Heights added to the slaughter.

Colonel Lee's vantage point, where he could plainly see the effects of his fire, and where he and his batterymen stood as targets for enemy long-range shelling from across the Antietam as well as from the field pieces Hooker was able to bring to bear on this side of the creek, caused him to remember the place as "artillery Hell."

This position was eventually overrun by Brigadier General George S. Greene's division of the XII Corps in a fight that saw some of Lee's guns—which had been placed in a forward position near the Mumma farm—seized by the charging Federals. Colonel Lee was ordered to fall back from here to Hauser Ridge, a southern extension of Nicodemus Heights. where his remaining guns continued to take a deadly toll.

2. DUNKER CHURCH

In 1851 the Mumma family donated a tract of land near their farm for the construction of a building so that they and fellow members of the congregation of the German Baptist Brethren would have a place to worship. The tract was at the intersection of the Hagerstown Pike and Smoketown Road, and two years later the small, brick building was completed. It was whitewashed and without ornamentation, as their simple beliefs even considered steeples presumptuous.

Worship services included washing the feet of neighbors and serving lamb stew to commemorate the Last Supper, with all members eating from the same dish to demonstrate a humble oneness. They also advocated baptism by complete immersion, from which they came to be called "Dunkers," or "Dunkards."

On Sunday, September 14, 1862, the Sharpsburg congregation met at the church, as they did every Sunday, but this day was different. The church members, whose faith followed the dictates of pacifism and simplicity, were undoubtedly abuzz over the threatening news of great

Dunker Church

armies marching in their midst. By that afternoon their fears were realized as they heard the distant thunder of artillery on South Mountain and saw battle smoke clouding the sky over the mountain passes.

The small congregation could little know what Fate had in store for their modest meeting house, which was to become the focal point of Joe Hooker's opening attack in the Battle of Antietam.

CONFEDERATE TROOPS POSTED at the Dunker Church and in the adjacent West Woods at dawn on the 17th—some 8,000 men—were under the command of perhaps the war's strangest soldier-Christian, Stonewall Jackson. Brigadier General John R. Jones' division, Jackson's old command, occupied the West Woods above the church, with Brigadier General Alexander R. Lawton's division extending east across David Miller's farm and the Samuel Mumma farm. Lawton had only recently assumed command of the division from Major General Richard S. Ewell, whose leg was shattered at Second Manassas.

Attached to Jackson's command for the impending battle, out of convenience rather than design, was Hood's division of Longstreet's Corps; these were hard-bitten Texans and others of the Deep South who had earned a reputation as tough fighters. The man at their head, John Bell Hood, had entered Maryland at the rear of the column—the post of one under arrest.

Hood had squabbled with his superiors over prizes won at Second Manassas, in this case several fine Federal ambulances. He was declared insubordinate and placed at the end of his column, without a command, but near enough to be elevated again for a battle: all part of the exasperating politics of soldier's honor, military protocol, and real necessity, which Lee endured stoically. (Hood regained his post during the South Mountain fighting.)

On the eve of battle, Hood's men had bivouacked in the woods behind the Dunker Church, and together with two brigades of Lawton's division, north of the church, served as a reserve during the opening attacks. Here they waited for any order to launch out of their woodland cover to plug a gap or exploit an advantage.

Just before Hooker's attack, Hood's men had been hoping to cook the rations that had been delivered around daybreak. Near 7:00 a.m. their breakfast was interrupted by an order to go to Lawton's aid. Half-eaten meals were left behind, and by 7:00, Hood's men were advancing out of the woods, across the turnpike, and, with a Rebel Yell, into a cornfield already littered with the battle's first dead and wounded. Hood had difficulty maneuvering his horse over and around fallen comrades. The first volley from his division staggered the Federal advance and pushed it back almost to the North Woods.

A SHORT TIME LATER the counterattack of Mansfield's XII Corps forced Hood back to the Dunker Church in see-saw fighting that characterized the bloody struggle in Miller's cornfield. The spearhead of Mansfield's advance, Brigadier General George S. Greene's division, pushed its line to within 200 yards of the Dunker Church, and a green regiment, the 125th Pennsylvania, found itself ordered to move from its protected rear position to seize the woods

around the church. They poured across the pike and
seized the church and surrounding woods.

Grave concern had earlier gripped the 125th's commander, Colonel Jacob Higgins, as he realized his position
near the church was one of apparent seclusion, devoid of
support from other XII Corps units. At about this time too,
Hooker rode close to the church to lay claim to his
achieved objective when a bullet struck him in the foot. He
left the field slightly injured, but content in victory.

Soon Higgins' concerns were dealt a blow of confirmation as McLaws' Rebel division came on the scene with a
yell and a volley, and was soon reinforced by troops of
Lawton's command. The churchyard and nearby woods
were cleared of Federals as the 125th was overwhelmed
and caught in a crossfire.

Greene's Union division, this time in force, again
attacked the Dunker Church after delivering a surprise
volley into the approaching enemy from a concealed
position east of the pike. Now it was the Yankees' turn to
yell, and the Union division surged across the pike, past
the church, and continued several hundred yards into the
woods beyond. To bolster his foothold, Greene scraped
together any available loose units, in particular the 13th
New Jersey and two pieces of artillery. Further comfort
was enjoyed as Major General John Sedgwick's division of
the II Corps came in sight, heading for the West Woods.

General Greene's was the deepest penetration of the
enemy's lines all morning and, in the knowledge that
Sedgwick's division was holding a position on his right
flank, Greene was determined to hold his position, or,

better yet, advance it. But the undoing of his hopes was that Sedgwick's attack into the woods north of him had been repulsed. Greene was suddenly attacked on both flanks, and again the ground around the Dunker Church was yielded to the Confederates. His attackers were troops of Brigadier General John G. Walker's division, shifted from the Snavely's Ford/Lower Bridge vicinity to assist the hard-pressed Confederate left.

But the Dunker Church grounds were not yet to be figured out of the fighting. Franklin's VI Corps had just arrived from Pleasant Valley (between South Mountain and Elk Ridge) and had taken position near the East Woods and Mumma farm, arriving in time to see Greene's men driven from the church area with screaming Rebels in hot pursuit. Union batteries opened "with a tornado of canister," halting the Confederates and sending the survivors reeling back to the shelter of the West Woods.

To discourage any further counterattack, VI Corps division commander Major General William F. "Baldy" Smith sent a brigade forward to the Mumma farm. But the brigade's commander, Colonel William H. Irwin, exceeded his orders and sent several regiments charging across the Mumma property, over Colonel Lee's former artillery position (grounds of the current Visitor Center), and into the near point-blank fire of the Confederates, who had taken cover in the woods around the church. Irwin fell back, considerably bloodied, ending the fighting in the West Woods sector.

AFTER THE BATTLE the damaged Dunker Church served as a hospital. It was not until 1864 that the congregation could repair the structure and resume services. In 1916 a new church was built in Sharpsburg proper and the old meeting house remained empty until 1921 when it fell prey to a violent storm. Reconstruction efforts were undertaken in 1960 and the rebuilt structure, containing original bricks, window frames, floorboards and furnishings, was dedicated in September 1962, on the 100th Anniversary of the battle. Even the church's Bible, "borrowed" after the battle by Sergeant Nathan Dykeman of the 107th New York (XII Corps), was returned to the congregation in 1903, and is now displayed at the Visitor Center.

3. JOSEPH POFFENBERGER FARM/NORTH WOODS

Joe Hooker's corps camped the night of September 16-17, on the farmland of Joseph Poffenberger, one of several Poffenbergers—Samuel, John and Alfred—in the neighborhood. (Samuel's farm, northeast of the scene of battle, was least affected by the battle's destruction, but Alfred's farm, near the West Woods/Dunker Church area, like Joseph's, was well in the path of battle lines.)

Similar to most farmers in the area, Joseph Poffenberger maintained a woodlot primarily to supply him with firewood, but occasionally for building material. The relative self-sufficiency of the nineteenth century family almost demanded such set-asides of otherwise useful farm ground. There are probably no more famous woodlots in American history than Antietam's East, West and North woods. It warrants mention that the three Antietam woodlots were considerably larger in 1862 than they are today.

Joseph Poffenberger's woods, soon to be dubbed the North Woods, was the smallest of the three woodlots and separated his farmhouse from the property of David Miller's to the south. Behind the screen of the North Woods and a rise of ground on the Poffenberger farm, Hooker went into bivouac on the eve of battle, grumbling that if McClellan had started the columns earlier their work might already be done. He was later severely critical of McClellan's propensity toward the "slows," as Lincoln termed it, sharing the sentiments of other observers of the day. As well, time and study have yet failed to yield concessions in Little Mac's behalf.

AT DAWN ON THE 17TH—judged to have been at 5:43 a.m.—Hooker had his men in lines of battle behind the North Woods. Focusing on the little white church about a mile away, which some men mistook as a schoolhouse because of the absence of a steeple, Hooker intended for Doubleday's division—spearheaded by Brigadier General John Gibbon's "damned Black Hats," soon to be more widely known as the Iron Brigade—to advance down the Hagerstown Pike, their lines astride the pike and extending into Miller's cornfield.

Brigadier General James B. Ricketts' lines formed the left of the assault column and extended beyond the East Woods, while George G. Meade's division formed the center, with Miller's cornfield directly in its path. At first light, with wisps of fog still clinging to the fields and swirling among the rows of tall corn in Miller's field, the divisions launched out from their cover and were greeted almost immediately by salvos from Colonel Lee's guns.

The Joseph Poffenberger farmhouse soon became full of the grisly by-products of the glory of advancing colors as the wounded and dying came streaming back by the hundreds, then more, as fighting ebbed and flowed across Miller's cornfield and its surrounding woodlots.

For many years it was accepted that Clara Barton came here while the battle was still raging and tended the wounded, and near this farmhouse was later placed a monument to her heroism, containing a red cross of bricks from her birthplace. However, new research points to the Samuel Poffenberger farm as the scene of her heroic mission. (The Samuel Poffenberger farm is included in Part II of the Antietam Tour.)

4. EAST WOODS

The East Woods was the scene of skirmishing on the evening of the 16th when Hood's division was sent forward to check Meade, who was screening the movements of the I Corps. As quick as the little fight flared—even artillery came into play—it subsided, and Hood pulled back to the Dunker Church, hoping to feed his hungry men who had not partaken of any real sustenance for three days.

Ricketts' division passed through the East Woods during the opening assault next morning. As his troops emerged from the woods, the crossfire from Rebel batteries near the Dunker Church and Pelham's horse artillery on Nicodemus Heights took a deadly toll, and the situation worsened as out of the smoke came the Louisiana Tigers as fresh support for Lawton's other regiments. A Federal battery was wrestled forward, converging fire from the cornfield came to bear, and the situation seemed to balance itself as neither side was able to achieve an advantage. The Confederates eventually fell back to the West Woods.

The 12th Massachusetts lost 67 percent of its numbers in the fight, a record among Union regiments at Antietam, while the brigade of Louisianians that faced them lost 61 percent. The loss concentrated on the men of the 12th might have been prevented had Ricketts coordinated a solid front, rather than the successive attacks by brigades, which resulted from maneuvering into position somewhat diagonally through the East Woods. Another factor was the large number of "good Samaritans" seen leaving the ranks to escort wounded comrades to the rear. An observer called it a "sorry sight" that so many able-bodied men would shirk their duty under the false pretense of humanitarianism.

Next came Hood's attack across Miller's field to the very edge of the woods, which fell, again, on only one of Ricketts' brigades, that of Colonel William A. Christian, and in particular one regiment, the 90th Pennsylvania under Colonel Peter Lyle. Ricketts' division ceased to be effective and moved to the rear.

But the East Woods would next be swept by the XII Corps' advance, Greene's division the spearhead, moving southwesterly through the woods. As the XII Corps approached the East Woods along the Smoketown Road, its commander, Joseph K. F. Mansfield, fell mortally wounded and was carried to the George Line house behind the lines; Brigadier General Alpheus S. Williams then assumed command of the corps.

A short time after the passage of the XII Corps, Sedgwick's division of Sumner's II Corps tramped a path due west through the bloodied forest, headed for its spirited but ill-fated attack on the West Woods.

5. MILLER'S CORNFIELD
or simply, "THE" CORNFIELD

More desperate fighting was concentrated in this 30-acre cornfield than anyplace else on the Antietam battlefield. Battle lines of various proportions see-sawed across it, leveling to the ground the man-tall stalks of corn, and earning it the distinction as "the" cornfield of the battle, if not the war. Raked by artillery fire from all four sides and tramped through by men from no fewer than a dozen different infantry divisions, Miller's cornfield was the bloodiest sector of the war's bloodiest day.

Joe Hooker later wrote: "In the time I am writing every stalk of corn in the northern and greater part of the field was cut as closely as could have been done with a knife, and the slain lay in rows precisely as they had stood in their ranks a few moments before. It was never my fortune to witness a more bloody, dismal battle-field." Hood's report of the battle called it the war's "most terrific clash of arms, by far."

Rufus Dawes served in the 6th Wisconsin—one of those "damned Black Hat" regiments. Those units had faced their first fire only three weeks before and were now in their third battle, each time pitted, coincidentally, against Stonewall Jackson's men. Dawes gave a vivid account of the cornfield fight:

Joe Hooker

Miller's Cornfield

John Bell Hood

After a few rods of advance, the line stopped and, by common impulse fell back to the edge of the corn and lay down on the ground behind the low rail fence. Another line of our men came up through the corn. We all joined together, jumped over the fence, and again pushed out into the open field.

There is a rattling fusillade and loud cheers. "Forward" is the word. The men are loading and firing with demoniacal fury and shouting and laughing hysterically, and the whole field before us is covered with rebels fleeing for life, into the woods. Great numbers of them are shot while climbing over the high post and rail fences along the turnpike. We push on over the open fields half way to the little church. . . .

A long and steady line of rebel gray, unbroken by the fugitives who fly before us, comes sweeping down through the woods around the church. They raise the yell and fire. It is like a scythe running through our line. . . . It is a race for life that each man runs for the cornfield. A sharp cut, as of a switch, stings the calf of my leg as I run. Back to the corn, and back through the corn, and headlong flight continues. . . .

This was the most dreadful slaughter to which our regiment was subjected in the war.

Recap by division (corps) of the cornfield fighting (Union corps are represented by Roman numerals):

- Doubleday (I) and Meade (I) advance from the north.

- Lawton (Jackson) with support from J. R. Jones (Jackson) meets attack from the south.

- Ricketts (I) feels his way through the East Woods and advances piecemeal from the northeast.

- Hood (Longstreet—Jackson) sweeps into the cornfield from the south and southwest.

- Williams (XII) and Greene (XII) come into the fight from the north and northeast.

- Elements of D. H. Hill's (Jackson) division, posted along a sunken road south of the Mumma farm, advances to support hard-pressed Confederates in the cornfield, but are thrown back by Greene's (XII) attack.

- Sedgwick's (II) flank passes through the cornfield approaching from due east to attack the West Woods, but is routed by the surprise counterattack of McLaws (Longstreet), Walker (Longstreet), and G. T. Anderson's brigade of D. R. Jones' (Longstreet) division, elements of which pursue the Federals back across the cornfield.

And the fighting in this sector was not over yet. Sedgwick's attack on the West Woods above the Dunker Church would close the morning phase of fighting at Antietam.*

6. WEST WOODS

A little after 9:00 a.m., while Miller's cornfield lay a smoldering, blood-drenched thirty acres of twisted bodies and moaning wounded, the next disjointed Union assault

---

* Of minor consequence to the great carnage harvested in Miller's cornfield that day, though worthy of mention, is the very name by which history has remembered this historic landmark. New findings by Betty Otto of the National Park Service tend to indicate that Mr. David Miller had no middle initial, thus the common reference "D.R." Miller's cornfield may be incorrect. (Miller family descendants insist there are no records of a middle initial.) Contentions are that the misnomer arose from Miller's patented "sure-fire" medicines, or home remedies, from which he became referred to locally, and perhaps somewhat tongue-in-cheek, as a "doctor"; hence, "Dr." Miller, not necessarily "D.R." Miller.

was building as John Sedgwick's division of the II Corps came onto the field. The I and XII corps had not attacked in concert; now the II Corps would follow suit, and again the common foot-soldier would be victimized by high command blundering. McClellan had lapsed into his cautious, jerky, defensive state of mind, and committed his troops to battle in what Sumner called "driblets."

The II Corps had been kept east of Antietam Creek until the morning of the 17th when McClellan finally gave the order to advance, unleashing the unbridled enthusiasm of the fighting-spirited and aged Edwin V. "Bull" Sumner, who had been pacing behind the lines anxiously waiting for the youngster McClellan to give the word. The corps crossed the creek at Pry's Ford, just south of the Upper Bridge, with Sedgwick's division the vanguard and Sumner personally on hand to direct the action.

In his enthusiasm, Sumner outdistanced his next division coming behind (Brigadier General William H. French's), reached the front well before his other divisions had time to come into sight, and impatiently plunged forward with only Sedgwick's troops. They passed through the East Woods and headed across the littered fields and meadows for the West Woods and what Sumner thought was beyond the shattered flank of the enemy, hoping then to wheel south and roll up the Confederate line. Enjoying the easiest advance yet across the terrible cornfield, Sumner felt reassured.

Suddenly Pelham's artillery opened in his face; the guns had moved south from Nicodemus Heights to its lower extension, Hauser Ridge, directly behind the West Woods. Sedgwick's lead brigade under Brigadier General

Willis A. Gorman plowed ahead through the woods and emerged into the fields of Alfred Poffenberger's farm, at the foot of Hauser Ridge, where Pelham's guns were posted. Also in the vicinity was a loose collection of survivors of the Stonewall Brigade that had taken position near Poffenberger's house, and Brigadier General Jubal A. Early's brigade posted off in the woods to their right.

NOTE: This point can be reached by following current Starke Avenue to its intersection with "new" Hagerstown Pike—MD Rt. 65, which bypasses the historical stretch of road within the park area—and entering the woods on the west side of the road. But only to the fenceline, please, as it is private property beyond.

As previously mentioned under the Dunker Church section, it was at this time that the isolated 125th Pennsylvania was swept out of the Dunker Church area by a sudden attack by McLaws' Confederate division. The Pennsylvanians were only the first unit to receive the shock of this counterattack that would fall heavily on Sedgwick's exposed flank in the upper West Woods. Hindered in maneuver by the woods and the narrow valley on the Alfred Poffenberger farm (which was commanded by Pelham's guns and those of Colonel S. D. Lee, recently pulled back from the plateau near the Hagerstown Pike/Smoketown Road intersection), Sedgwick had little hope of turning to meet the surprise attack head-on.

McLaws' division, which had rested in the fields behind Lee's headquarters (in an oak grove west of town), handily marched cross-country to arrive in the nick of time to bolster the left, as had Walker's division from Snavely's Ford on the far right. More than 2,000 Union soldiers became casualties of the attack in less than half an hour, and in their retreat from the West Woods the bloody cornfield again saw action as pursuing Confederates chased them back to the East Woods and beyond. The shattered I Corps and a large part of the bloodied XII Corps had already retreated to the East Woods, licking their wounds, resolute that the battle was over for them, and thus ending the morning phase at Antietam.

7. SAMUEL MUMMA (MOO´-ma) HOUSE SITE

When battle was joined just after daybreak, the Samuel Mumma house was already a casualty. Men of D. H. Hill's Confederate division, posted along a sunken road about 700 yards south of the Mumma farm, had drawn upon their past battle experience and resolved that the nearby farmhouse was a potential sniper's nest for the enemy. Therefore it was burned to the ground. (One of its outbuildings survived, and still does to this day, as does the Mumma cemetery which contains 336 graves; the house was later rebuilt.)

8. MUMMA FARM—ROULETTE FARM

The Mumma farm and neighboring Roulette farm were traversed by troops marching to the scene of battle during the morning phase of fighting, but are more closely associated with the midday phase, as two divisions of Sumner's II Corps plodded through the fields and meadows seeking an unseen enemy.

As noted earlier, John Sedgwick's division had led Sumner's corps onto the field considerably ahead of the next following division, French's. Sumner's third division, under Major General Israel B. Richardson, had temporarily been held east of the creek by McClellan for, as one might expect, defensive measures, until an adequate force could be moved up to take its position. Well over an hour later a division of Major General Fitz John Porter's V Corps filled the spot in the mighty reserve line, and Richardson finally took off after the rest of the II Corps.

TWO PRINCIPAL ANALYSTS of the Battle of Antietam, James V. Murfin and Stephen W. Sears, seem to be at odds as to how the next phase developed. Sears contends that when French reached the East Woods and Sedgwick was not in sight—having already moved out quickly under Sumner's personal direction to assault the West Woods—French halted a puzzled moment, spied Greene's XII Corps division holding the plateau near the Dunker Church, and decided on his own to support Greene's flank. He wheeled south and marched off, innocently or otherwise, to achieve his objective.

Murfin, on the other hand, attributes French's shift of the battle to accident, interpreting no blame on French for the change of direction. According to Murfin, French followed Sedgwick intending to swing in along the latter's flank, but ran into D. H. Hill's pickets and "unconsciously turned the axis of the battle." It should be noted that the terrain in the vicinity of the lower East Woods/Mumma Farm/Roulette Farm contains a series of dips and rises, which depending on one's vantage point conceal sections of the field of fight. French's decision may have been guided by what panorama was presented to him from the geographical point of his arrival.

In any event, French headed south unsupported across the Mumma farm and past the Roulette house (his march roughly parallel to the park road leading away from the Mumma house site) over unfamiliar ground toward an uncertain fate. Sedgwick was already somewhere on the field, but French knew not precisely where; and even less was known of the other II Corps division, Richardson's men, who, in fact, were just getting their feet wet crossing Antietam Creek.

Skirmishers were encountered around the Roulette house but were dealt with handily and the lines advanced without stuttering a step—except a short time later when some bee hives on the Roulette farm were disturbed by a Confederate shell. This caused some disruption in the 132nd Pennsylvania as the men found themselves attacked by angry bees.

Ahead lay a gentle rise of ground that beyond its crest descended just as gently for a short distance. It then dropped abruptly several feet into a sunken farm road between the Roulette and Henry Piper farms, where the Confederates were waiting, poised to deliver their first crushing volley.

9. THE SUNKEN ROAD, or BLOODY LANE

Posted in this road, partially concealed from view, was the bulk of D. H. Hill's Confederate division: the brigade of Brigadier General Robert E. Rodes, occupying the western stretch of road, and Brigadier General George B. Anderson's brigade, holding the portion of the road beyond its slight bend at Roulette's Lane. (The stretch of

Israel Richardson

D. H. Hill

Bloody Lane

road, preserved and maintained by the park service—where the interpretive markers are placed and the observation tower is located—was Anderson's section of road.)

As the van of French's division—Brigadier General Max Weber's untried three-regiment brigade (1st Delaware, 5th Maryland, and 4th New York)—came over the rise, Hill's men staggered them with a powerful volley delivered at a range of less than 100 yards. Colonel John B. Gordon, who was commanding the 6th Alabama of Rodes' brigade, later wrote of the opening volley:

The effect was appalling. The entire front line, with few exceptions, went down in the consuming blast. Before the rear lines could recover, my exultant men were on their feet, devouring them with successive volleys. The fight now became furious, and deadly.

The desperate struggle continued as French committed his other two brigades and exultant Rebels actually left the cover of the road and made stand-up efforts at counterattacking, only to be driven back. And despite the Confederates' advantage of cover, French's numbers exceeded the Confederate count by more than two-to-one, so that his men were delivering, as well as receiving, crushing volleys. The farm road was soaked with blood as Confederates were struck and knocked out of line, forming neat rows of dead men in the road behind them.

Because of the nature of their cover, most of the Rebels had upper body or head wounds. The 6th Alabama's Colonel Gordon was shot five times, the last one in the face, but was spared from drowning in his own blood only because his hat, into which he'd fallen face down, had a

George B. Anderson, mortally wounded at Antietam.

Confederate dead in Bloody Lane. The photo was taken on September 19.

bullet hole through it, allowing the blood to drain out. After September 17, this hitherto anonymous sunken road would be remembered as Bloody Lane.

NEXT ON THE SCENE was Richardson's division, following the sound of the guns and arriving just in time to add its weight to the attack, and in position to strike the Rebel right flank. French's men, however, were already spent, so it would be another unfortunate piecemeal attack.

On the Confederate side, Major General Richard H. Anderson's division of Longstreet's Corps, which started the day in reserve near Lee's headquarters west of Sharpsburg, was rushed to the Piper farm below the Sunken Road. Artillery there, growing in number as more guns were run to this front, extracted a deadly toll virtually unanswered by Yankee guns, most of which were still on the other side of the Antietam, the gunners fearful of hitting their own men.

Richardson's division included the famed Irish Brigade under Brigadier General Thomas F. Meagher and its own famous "Fighting 69th" New York; with their emerald flag whipping overhead, all charged headlong into the fight. The Confederate right collapsed under the attack and carried with it the rest of the Sunken Road line as Union troops, those spilling into the road and others occupying the bordering ridge, had a clear line of fire into the Southern ranks.

Only a desperate counterattack by Hill's depleted ranks and Anderson's reinforcements—the former commencing the operation with an abrupt "ATTENTION . . .

CHARGE!'"—were the Confederates able to regain their position and discourage the two Federal divisions from further attacks.

The tide-turning was gained principally by the superiority in numbers of artillery the Confederates were able to bring to bear at the point of attack. This was a sad realization for French's and Richardson's Union divisions, which fought at Bloody Lane without any appreciable artillery support, when McClellan had nearly 300 guns at his disposal.

The fighting at Bloody Lane—Antietam's midday phase—lasted three and a half hours (from about 9:30 a.m. to nearly 1:00 p.m.), costing the Confederates more than 2,500 men, including General George B. Anderson, who was mortally wounded. Union casualties amounted to almost 3,000, including the mortally wounded General Richardson. As things quieted here, with the day's combined casualty toll already inching up toward 19,000 of the 60,000 engaged so far, the afternoon phase took shape at the Lower Bridge where Ambrose Burnside began seriously to force a crossing of the Antietam.

10. BURNSIDE BRIDGE

The most well-known landmark of the Antietam battlefield is Burnside Bridge, and easily the first impression gained from a visit to the place is total contempt for the generalship of Ambrose E. Burnside, the kind, well-intentioned, sometimes pouting Federal commander charged with forcing a crossing of the Antietam here. Built in 1836 and originally known as the Lower, or Rohrbach

Bridge, after Burnside left his indelible mark on this part of the battlefield it came to be called Burnside Bridge, a dubious honor at best. While a strong case against Burnside's handling of his objective can be readily formulated, even by the most casual battlefield tourist who wanders down the trail to inspect the bridge and read the interpretive plaques, in all fairness to the general, other factors should be considered that are not so obvious from a visit. These factors certainly do not exonerate Burnside from all blame, but they do mitigate the case to a degree, and uncover certain roots leading back to—where else?—McClellan's headquarters.

For most of the morning and midday fighting, Burnside and his IX Corps had remained idle, watching the battle rage on other parts of the field; they had a particularly fine view directly down the Sunken Road as the two lines collided there, then became enveloped in smoke and muzzle flashes. Burnside was chafed after losing half his wing command—Hooker's corps—leaving him in an unacceptable sort of figure-head command. Brigadier General Jacob D. Cox was technically in command of the IX Corps, so orders were received by Burnside, who scanned them, then handed them over to Cox for execution—all to satisfy his link responsibility in the awkward chain of command.

Just after 9 a.m., when the battle was already three hours old, orders were written by McClellan to begin an attack on the bridge, but the orders were not received by Burnside until about 10 a.m. The orders stated that once a crossing of the Antietam was made and an advance underway, reinforcements would be sent from the Middle Bridge area to support his attack, presumably intended

Ambrose E. Burnside

Burnside Bridge

by McClellan to prevent Lee from drawing strength from this section to meet attacks elsewhere (which Lee was ultimately able to accomplish with outstanding timeliness and effect). Thus, a late go-ahead from McClellan was working against Burnside. Next came the natural obstacles of terrain, and the problems of maneuver in the face of a protected, hostile presence.

LEE'S FORCES IN THE AREA of the Lower Bridge had already been critically drained to meet other attacks so that only a meager supply of manpower remained. But the Confederate troops—the 2nd and 20th Georgia regiments, some 400 men under Brigadier General Robert Toombs—were equal to the task, particularly because their position was highly defensible. They were posted on the wooded high ground overlooking the bridge and concealed in the woods along the creek where they could very effectively snipe at any enemy troops on the opposite bank, which for the most part was open ground. Another hundred Georgians (50th Georgia) and a handful of South Carolinians were posted farther downstream near a 90-degree bend in the creek.

Brigadier General Isaac Rodman's Federal division and a brigade under Colonel Hugh Ewing (of Colonel Eliakim Scammon's Kanawha Division) were sent downstream to cross the creek at a ford McClellan's engineers had discovered the day before, all in the hope of flanking the Confederates. The 11th Connecticut, acting as scouts and skirmishers to screen Rodman's march, were literally cut to pieces by enemy snipers. Counted among the casualties was the 11th's commander, Colonel Henry W. Kingsbury, who was mortally wounded. When Rodman's force reached the ford supposedly scouted by the engineers they found it impossible to cross.

The banks on both sides were steep, and the enemy side of the creek was wooded and infested with more snipers doing their deadly work, discouraging any thought of storming across at any point. Confounded, Rodman sent troops from the 8th Connecticut ahead to scout for another crossing. Thus, they set out to do the work of the cavalry, when most of the Union horsemen were idling away their time massed at the Middle Bridge waiting to deliver McClellan's master stroke, and some of whom, incredibly enough, were sleeping while the battle raged, lulled by the soporific effect of their long-range artillery passing overhead.

Meanwhile, Brigadier General James Nagle was selected to storm the bridge with his 2nd Maryland, 6th and 9th New Hampshire, and 48th Pennsylvania regiments. The avenue of attack, the Lower Bridge Road, exposed them to flank fire. Tremendous losses mounted with no bridgehead gained. Valuable time and many lives were being lost, Rodman was effectively out of the picture, and more orders came from headquarters demanding an attack on the Lower Bridge front.

It was about noon when Brigadier General Edward Ferrero formed the 51st New York and 51st Pennsylvania for another assault. This one was to come over and down the hill directly in front of the bridge entrance, so as not to repeat the tragedy of Nagle's attack along the open roadway. After a brief artillery barrage to pave the way, the two regiments darted for the bridge, but enemy fire blunted and split the column.

The New Yorkers scrambled for fence cover on the left side of the bridge, and the 51st Pennsylvania sought refuge behind a stone wall on the right. Then with a cheer, the two regiments stormed the bridge and the heights beyond.

An order to withdraw came down the Rebel line and the Georgians retreated, except a small detachment posted in the narrow peninsula below the bridge (now called Georgian Overlook). According to one account, they failed to receive the fall-back order and were later found slumped in rows where they had stood, shot dead from the rear as the Federal lines enveloped the place. (The possibility also exists that they may have been struck down accidentally by fire from their own men posted to their left rear.)

THE ORDERS ISSUED by McClellan at about 9 a.m. were not successfully achieved until near 1 p.m., about the time the Bloody Lane fighting subsided, and precious hours had been lost to the Union effort as a meager force of Georgians had held an entire corps at bay. The criticism most commonly heaped upon Burnside is that the creek could have been waded at many points near the bridge and should not have been regarded as a major obstacle against forming the IX Corps in battle lines and splashing across in force. Indeed, Colonel Henry Kyd Douglas of Stonewall Jackson's staff, who was a native of the area and the chief source for providing information about the Antietam's wartime water levels, later wrote:

Go look at it and tell me if you don't think Burnside and his corps might have executed a hop, skip, and jump and landed on the other side. One thing is certain, they might have waded it that day without getting their waist belts wet in any place. Why Burnside's Bridge? Is it sarcasm?

If Burnside could have perceived his objective with the urgency required and launched such a bold stroke he could well have been the hero of Antietam; however, his listlessness and pouting precluded aggressive behavior that day. And would not McClellan himself, who dictated the over-cautious and very conservative stance for the army, have counseled against an attack that provided no safe avenue of retreat and didn't immediately provide for the convenient advance of artillery and supply, which required bridges or fords?

McClellan was one observer who had mixed feelings about Burnside's performance. In his October 15, 1862, report of the battle he graphically described the obstacles confronting Burnside, leaving the impression that he felt the commander had made the most of a difficult situation:

The valley of the Antietam at and near this bridge is narrow, with high banks. On the right of the stream the bank is wooded, and commands the approaches both to the bridge and the ford. The steep slopes of the bank were lined with rifle-pits and breastworks of rails and stones. These, together with the woods, were filled with the enemy's infantry, while their batteries completely commanded and enfiladed the bridge and ford and their approaches.

The advance of the troops brought on an obstinate and sanguinary contest, and, from the great natural advantages of the position, it was nearly 1 o'clock before the heights on the right bank were carried.

However, in his August 1863 report McClellan, now the deposed commander, was highly critical of Burnside. He mentioned the prodding required to get Burnside to advance, concluding with: "If this important movement had been consummated two hours earlier . . . victory might thus have been much more decisive."

One way to analyze the Union debacle at Burnside Bridge is to reverse some roles. If Burnside had been charged with holding the bridge with some 500 men and, say, Stonewall Jackson was ordered to force a crossing with his corps, would it have taken four hours? Further, would Lee have waited so late in the day to order an assault? And would the crossing points of the Antietam have gone unscouted by his cavalry? Perhaps Burnside earned his dubious distinction, but Little Mac should at least have a ford named for him.

11. SNAVELY'S FORD

Snavely's Ford is reached by a 2.5-mile-long trail along the west bank of the Antietam, beginning at the foot of Burnside Bridge. Taking the trail offers insight to the obstacles confronting Rodman's troops. The west bank is very steep in places and wooded all along, offering convenient snipers' nests, while the east bank is also steep in a few places, but was mostly cleared at the time of the battle. Just past the sharp bend in the creek, about three-quarters of a mile downstream, is the fording place supposedly scouted by McClellan's engineers.

When General Rodman's flanking force discovered it could not cross at the ford below the bend in the Antietam,

Snavely's Ford

two companies of the 8th Connecticut were ordered to follow the creek in search of another crossing. A place called Snavely's Ford was known to exist but had not been thoroughly scouted by the IX Corps or the cavalry or McClellan's engineers. When it was finally located the march had taken Rodman well around to the left and his troops were unable to get across the creek until Burnside Bridge had been stormed.

Attached to Rodman's force that day was Colonel Hugh Ewing's brigade consisting of the 12th, 23rd, and 30th Ohio regiments. Counted among the ranks of the 23rd Ohio were two men destined for the White House: Lieutenant Colonel Rutherford B. Hayes, who was wounded at South Mountain and replaced by Major James M. Comly, and Commissary Sergeant William McKinley, who would be heralded for serving rations to the men, under fire, after they had gained a foothold on the Sharpsburg side of the creek. An imposing monument to McKinley stands on the bluffs above Burnside Bridge. McKinley's meritorious conduct as a commissary sergeant contains a hint of Burnside's next delay.

12. THE FINAL ASSAULT

After the successful storming of Burnside Bridge at about 1 p.m., new problems were encountered. The victorious troops, men of Ferrero's brigade followed by the remnants of Nagle's brigade (which had made the first unsuccessful attempt), all part of Brigadier General Samuel D. Sturgis' division, were low on ammunition. Also, Brigadier General Orlando B. Willcox's fresh division, the only other IX Corps division not yet across the creek, had not been ordered up to the front and was still back near the Rohrbach house, almost a mile away.

An hour was wasted for Willcox's division to reach the bridge; another hour was lost in getting it across and into position. The whole division was forced, under Burnside's direction, to cross at the bridge rather than wade the shallow, uncontested creek.

Earlier, Colonel George Crook's brigade, part of Scammon's Kanawha Division holding a position up-stream from the bridge—near where a modern bridge now carries the redirected Lower Bridge Road across the Antietam and past the Otto and Sherrick houses, so as to close off traffic at Burnside Bridge—discovered that indeed the Antietam was shallow and waded across, becoming the only IX Corps troops (besides Rodman's expedition) to get their feet wet.

This delay was entirely the fault of Burnside, and more so than not wading the creek to storm the heights, and not properly scouting the area, was his most serious error of neglect this day. He had established his bridgehead, but the delay in launching his attack frittered away valuable hours, permitting time for A. P. Hill's Confederate division, hard-marching from Harper's Ferry, to reach the battlefield.

Meanwhile, many of the Union soldiers already across the creek sat down to boil coffee, others were distributed rations, and some caught cat-naps, disturbed only by the nagging fire from Toombs' Georgians—who had fallen back to the protection of a stone wall a half-mile away—and occasional shelling from Confederate batteries.

With Rodman on the left and Willcox on the right, and Ewing's and Crook's brigades of the Kanawha Division thrown in for good measure, the IX Corps—some 12,000 strong—lurched forward at about 3 p.m. with nothing between them and Sharpsburg but Toombs' remnant and about 3,000 men of Brigadier General David R. Jones' division. The latter was posted along the Harper's Ferry Road, with its lines stretching across the southeast edge of town to the hill where the National Cemetery (Cemetery Hill) is now located.

Willcox encountered resistance near the Otto and Sherrick farms, and was dealt severe blows from enemy artillery on Cemetery Hill where Rebel cannoneers worked their guns virtually unmolested by Union batteries. Nevertheless, Willcox continued to advance at a deliberate pace, dislodged snipers from the Sherrick house, and soon a Massachusetts battery was run out to the Otto house.

General Rodman, on the left, advanced with equal determination, pushing Colonel Edward Harland's brigade of predominately Connecticut regiments into a 40-acre cornfield, while Colonel Harrison S. Fairchild's brigade of New Yorkers pressed forward across plowed fields on the right. Between Rodman and Willcox was the resupplied division under Sturgis, depleted from its storming of the bridge, but there to offer its weight as a reserve force to bolster the center, and ready to plug any gap.

James Murfin in *The Gleam of Bayonets* quotes Confederate private John Dooley (1st Virginia Regiment, Brigadier General James Kemper's brigade), who was posted in the aforementioned cornfield before Rodman's advance and watched the blue hordes gather before him:

In the field below us the enemy are slowly but cautiously approaching, crouching low as they advance behind the undulating tracks in the rich meadows through which they are passing. From the numbers of their flags which are distinctly visible above the rising ground we judge them to be at least two thousand in number.

After two artillery pieces on the extreme right flank of the Confederate line were knocked out by Union battery fire, Private Dooley expressed his apprehensions:

We were now left to oppose the numerous masses before us with a mere picket line of musketry. There may have been other troops to our left and right but I did not see any. The Yankees, finding no batteries opposing them, approach closer and closer, cowering down as near to the ground as possible . . . [then] they rise up and make a charge for our fence. Hastily emptying our muskets into their lines, we fled back through the cornfield.

Oh, how I ran! or tried to run through the high corn . . . I was afraid of being struck in the back, and I frequently turned half around in running so as to avoid if possible so disgraceful a wound.

The Confederate right was in dire straits and many of its defenders were already scrambling back through the streets of Sharpsburg, where confusion reigned as panicked soldiers mingled with hastily drawn guns, caissons and wagons. Adding to the discomfort, McClellan had finally pushed Brigadier General George Sykes' Regulars of the V Corps across the Middle Bridge, along with part of the heretofore inactive cavalry—more than 4,000 troopers in total—under Brigadier General Alfred Pleasonton, who, coupled with Willcox's advance, scattered the Cemetery Hill defenders into the Sharpsburg confusion.

Rodman, on the far left of the Union advance, continued his progress, but two regiments got left behind in the cornfield due to a mixup in orders, and only the 8th Connecticut emerged from the opposite side of the field, advancing unsupported as the flank regiment of the assault. The regiment charged for the Harper's Ferry Road and three enemy guns that had just wheeled into place on the ridge. General Rodman was riding near the front when he spied enemy troops approaching his exposed flank. He had no sooner sent a warning to his troops in the cornfield than a bullet tore into his chest, inflicting a mortal wound.

GENERAL LEE HAD WATCHED the collapse of his right but was unruffled by impending disaster. At 2:30 p.m. he had been advised that A. P. Hill's division from Harper's Ferry was crossing the Potomac at Boteler's Ford only three miles west of Sharpsburg. Literally at the point of Hill's sword his Light Division had made the 17-mile march in less than eight hours, at the cost of leaving much of its strength strung out along the road. Nevertheless, Hill's men would be arriving just at the right time and place.

From a rise of ground Lee watched the blue lines surging across the fields above the Lower Bridge and pushing toward the Harper's Ferry Road. Then, sometime before 4 p.m., a column of troops was seen approaching Lee's right by the road leading from Miller's sawmill on the bank of the Potomac. Turning to a nearby battery officer, Lieutenant John Ramsey, who had a telescope, Lee asked him to identify the troops.

The lieutenant handed the glass to Lee, but the general indicated he couldn't hold it—the result of having two bandaged hands: one broken wrist and the other badly sprained from a freak fall early in the campaign. The lieutenant ran his glass over the landscape toward the far right, spied a column of troops, and told Lee they were flying the United States flag.*

Author James Murfin cites the account of Rhode Island lieutenant colonel Joseph R. Curtis, which states in part: "As the enemy showed the national flag, and as our troops had been seen in advance on our right, moving diagonally across the front, the order to cease firing was given, and a volunteer officer to go forward to ascertain who was in our front was called for."

From this, one might believe Lieutenant Ramsey had focused on Stars and Stripes-carrying Confederates. However, author Stephen Sears contends that the Rhode Islanders had seen the colors of the 1st South Carolina— one of the regiments of Brigadier General Maxcy Gregg's leading brigade—which was very similar to the U.S. flag.

Whatever troops Ramsey had spied, Lee, not satisfied, asked him to focus again on another column. The answer was, "They are flying the Virginia and Confederate flags," to which Lee's casual and now famous reply, martially beautiful in its own simplicity and hardly reflective of the magnitude of the moment, was, "It is A. P. Hill from Harper's Ferry."

---

* As well, Longstreet had entered Maryland wearing a carpet slipper to protect a sore and blistered heel, and Jackson was badly bruised after being thrown from a new horse early in the campaign.

And so it was. Hill's men, some 3,300 troops—but not nearly the number on the field for attack, as many were still straggling along the road, breathless and footsore from their lightning march—crashed into the IX Corps' flank sometime between 3:30 and 4:00 p.m. The exposed 8th Connecticut was riddled with crossfire from front and flank. The Yankee lines wavered and fell back to the 40-acre cornfield, where much the same scene as that in Miller's field, earlier in the day, was repeated.

While the issue of the Confederates possibly carrying the U. S. flag may be debated, there is no question that some of the Southerners had exchanged their rags for new blue uniforms taken from the captured supplies at Harper's Ferry. Colonel Ewing's three Ohio regiments, thrown in on Rodman's left near the cornfield, were taken in by the advancing blue-clad Confederates of Gregg's brigade, were outflanked, caught a withering fire, and had to fall back.

J. T. Moore of the 30th Ohio later wrote:

When the line had advanced as far as the field of corn, the men were almost exhausted, and, for want of proper support, the left wing of the regiment was unprotected. General A. P. Hill's rebel division came down with crushing force on the exposed flank. . . . The national colors were torn in fourteen places by shot and shell. Both color bearers were killed. Sergeant White defiantly waved the flag in the face of the enemy until he was killed. Sergeant Carter, in his death agony, held the flagstaff so firmly that it could with difficulty be taken from his hand.

Coming onto the field as well, off Gregg's left, was a brigade of North Carolinians under Brigadier General

Lawrence O'Brien Branch, which pursued the fleeing Unionists down the ridge. But General Branch, riding at the front of his charging lines, was shot through the head and fell dead.

A. P. Hill arrived in the nick of time to save Lee's right and the day for the Confederacy. Hill's artillery, which had formed the van of his column, wheeled into battery and opened with telling effect on the IX Corps, and along with his spirited infantry attack ended the fighting at Antietam. With no real support on Burnside's right, which McClellan had promised to supply once a breakthrough was made, Burnside was forced to assume the defensive, performed remarkably well to salvage some order out of potential disaster, and rallied with his back to the Antietam.

Hill brought the rest of his division into line, stretching from near the Otto house to Snavely's Ford, where cavalry guarded his flank, anchored on Antietam Creek. But due to losses in his command, and content with having reestablished the army's right, no further attacks were initiated by Lee. Soon the sun set over the blood-drenched fields and farm lanes of the Antietam Valley, ending the war's bloodiest day.

13. ANTIETAM NATIONAL CEMETERY

On March 23, 1865, the state of Maryland provided for the establishment of the Antietam National Cemetery, an item of business negotiated as the Civil War was winding down to its final days. By then the fortunes of war in the East had gone against Lee, principally due to the emergence of Ulysses S. Grant, who possessed neither the martial appearance nor the text book brilliance of George B. McClellan, but who seldom failed to commit all his troops to battle or to exploit an advantage. By 1866 a stone wall around the cemetery was completed, followed in 1867 by the iron fence and gate, and the Lodge House just inside the entranceway. On September 17, 1880, the 18th Anniversary of the battle, the Antietam National Cemetery was dedicated. It contains 4,776 Federal dead, including 1,836 unknown soldiers.

Feelings still ran strong in the early postwar years. Henry Kyd Douglas related an interesting story of "Lee's Rock" within the grounds of the cemetery. It seems that when some trees were cleared away for the cemetery a large boulder was discovered, and rumor soon had it that Lee had stood upon the rock to watch the battle. This was entirely unacceptable to many people, who believed the sanctity of the resting place was tainted by including such a landmark of rebellion within the cemetery grounds. The extremists won out, and according to Douglas, "Lee's Rock was broken up; dug up, scattered, obliterated." He continued:

We former Rebels looked on, while the fury seethed, in silent amusement, and when it was all over, revealed the truth that Lee never saw the rock; if he had seen it he could not have climbed upon it [presumably because of his injured hands]; if he had done that he could not have seen anything on the outside of the trees. . . .

This concludes Part I.

Along Antietam Creek
September 17, 1862

Part II

The Introduction to Part II was written by the late James V. Murfin, author of THE GLEAM OF BAYONETS (1965). After the Introduction is an analysis of General George B. McClellan as the Union commander at Antietam. Stephen W. Sears, author of the highly acclaimed LANDSCAPE TURNED RED: THE BATTLE OF ANTIETAM (1983), and GEORGE B. McCLELLAN: THE YOUNG NAPOLEON (1988), has tackled this subject in "McClellan at Antietam," which serves as additional background before beginning the Driving Tour of Part II.

Introduction

by James V. Murfin

ANTIETAM WAS A STRANGE BATTLE and an interesting one, perhaps the most argued and discussed of the war. McClellan started with a plan designed to roll Lee into the Potomac with one massive, coordinated, three-pronged attack. Instead, he struck first with his right, then in the middle, then on the left. They were three unorganized, disjointed moves that gave Lee a chance to shift his troops wherever and whenever they were needed—a huge chess game of potentially mating moves by the men in blue that were checked every time by the men in gray.

One of McClellan's generals became angry because he couldn't go first, and, in a snit, refused to cooperate. McClellan himself became ill during the heat of battle and took to his bed. (Funny, he had the same illness at the height of battle only a few months before in Virginia.) Some officers felt McClellan was conducting the battle badly, yet he thought he was doing so well that some claimed he talked of marching on Washington and taking over the government.

While Lee waited patiently for all of his men to arrive from the Harper's Ferry expedition (some came on the field late in the morning), McClellan fought the battle with 25,000 fresh troops in the rear, never used, and he claimed he needed 50,000 more to face Lee's "100,000," a figure McClellan claimed until his death.

As the fighting see-sawed across the fields throughout the day, scores of small human dramas were acted out. There was the washer-woman that the famed Irish Brigade brought with them, who was seen following her Union boys almost to the battle line waving her hat and screaming, "Give 'em hell!"

During the advance of the 132nd Pennsylvania, a Confederate shell hit a colony of bee hives in the Roulette orchard. It was touch and go for awhile as the men ran for cover from an odd assortment of swarming bullets and bees. At the moment, the 132nd, a newly-recruited regiment, could not have cared less whether it was more humiliating to break under the sting of lead or bees.

The whole thing was a little too much for them. After considerable prodding by officers, the lines moved on to the high ground overlooking the Piper farm and the Sunken Road and out of danger, but these boys would never forget this incident. Long after time clouded their memories, long after battle lines and formations became sketchy images, they remembered their skirmish with the bees.

Clara Barton nursed at Antietam, and the Red Cross erected a monument to her efforts. But no one has seen fit to honor the 500 prostitutes who gave up the luxury of their plush surroundings in Washington to follow the Federal army to Boonsboro, where they established a "tent city."

Antietam was filled with items of human interest from the morning's opening shots to the last fading thunder of artillery at dusk. Novelists could not have written a more surprising and exciting ending. As McClellan had shifted his thrusts from the north to the south of his lines, accomplishing little more than wasting lives, Lee followed, holding on, hoping that the last division of his troops at Harper's Ferry, under fiery, red-bearded General Ambrose Powell Hill, might come up, some 3,000 men he desperately needed.

It was a long and agonizing wait, for throughout the afternoon it seemed that at any minute the whole Confederate line would collapse. At about four o'clock, an aide announced to General Lee that he had spotted some troops off in the distance. "They are flying the Virginia and Confederate flags, sir," the aide said. With a great sigh of relief, Lee calmly replied, "It is A. P. Hill from Harper's Ferry." When the news of reinforcements reached the line there was a mighty roar of happy voices. They dug in just a little harder.

At about three o'clock that afternoon, the Federal left, having at last crossed the bridge ultimately to carry the name of General Burnside, began to gain some momentum across the high ground to the south of Sharpsburg. It was painfully evident that unless a miracle was performed, the Confederates would be rolled up and, if not surrounded, at least pushed to the river with little chance of escape.

The 16th Connecticut and the 4th Rhode Island, both brand new outfits never before in battle, were carrying the extreme left wing when a most curious thing happened. A heavy volley of fire came across the cornfield from where, up to this point, there had been only a handful of the enemy.

It was A. P. Hill's division arriving just in the nick of time. They struck the left flank of Burnside's advance and forced the Federals back to the Antietam. Lee's right flank was reestablished and the bloody fighting at Antietam came to a close.

The day had been long. Battle had raged for nearly twelve hours. The men on both sides were weary, but still alert. The Confederates below Sharpsburg, particularly sensitive to the situation, prepared for a countercharge should it come. But it never came. The sun set and campfires were lit. As the sounds of battle slowly faded, screaming shells and musket rattle were replaced with the terrible moans of the wounded, the mournful cries of thousands who would not live to see daybreak.

Throughout the night, informal truces were set up between the lines so that medical attendants could bring their own back for treatment. Barns, chickenhouses, private homes, and churches, almost any building or shelter that was not occupied, were used for surgery, embalming stations, and make-shift hospitals, where the wounded, stacked like so many logs, waited for death.

Thursday came and went and, although Lee expected McClellan to attack, the Federal commander believed he was still outnumbered and could not fight again without reinforcements. That night the Army of Northern Virginia escaped across the river back to home territory.

Messages from Washington urged McClellan to pursue the retreating Confederates. But Little Mac said he was lacking in ammunition. His army had fought a hard battle and although he claimed a "complete" victory at

Antietam, by his estimation the army needed more time to refit. In early October, President Lincoln paid him a visit on the battlefield. Again Lincoln asked his general to cross the Potomac in pursuit of Lee. McClellan reported that his army's horses were "absolutely broken down from fatigue," and were "sore-tongued," lame, and had sore backs. "Will you pardon me for asking," Lincoln replied, "what the horses of your army have done since the battle of Antietam that fatigue anything?"

Official figures of the Army of the Potomac at the end of September showed 32,885 horses and mules available for duty and over 3,200 baggage and supply wagons in acceptable condition. Lincoln, in disgust, once referred to the huge Army of the Potomac as "McClellan's bodyguard."

"After the battle of Antietam, I went up to the field to try to get him to move and came back thinking he would move at once," Lincoln said. The President continued:

But when I got home he began to argue why he ought not to move. I preemptorily ordered him to advance. It was 19 days before he put a man over the river. It was nine days longer before he got his army across and then he stopped again, delaying on little pretexts of wanting this and that. I began to fear he was playing false—that he did not want to hurt the enemy. I saw how he could intercept the enemy on the way to Richmond, I determined to make that the test: If he let them get away I would remove him. He did so and I relieved him.

On November 7, 1862, Major General Ambrose E. Burnside took command of the Army of the Potomac.

ROBERT E. LEE WAS PROUD of his army at Antietam. Some say he considered this the finest battle he directed. He believed his men had shown their best against the greatest odds they ever encountered. He had done wonders; indeed, he had done what many would have considered impossible. With an army exhausted from battle and long marches, lacking in material strength, and with only a thin thread of hope to drive it on, Lee succeeded in bringing far greater damage to his opponent than he himself received.

The outcome of the Maryland Campaign cannot be based on physical damage alone, however, anymore than the question of victory or defeat at Sharpsburg can be resolved on the successful accomplishments of either army. Antietam is far more complex than this.

The Maryland Campaign began as a political and economic struggle: a fight by the Confederacy for the right to be left alone, to exist within its own boundaries. The Southern states were asking nothing more. Lee carried in his pocket this message to the people of the North. He was not invading to conquer, to occupy *per se*, but to demonstrate to the North and the world the determination with which his people were willing to fight for their independence.

When the Maryland Campaign ended, the Emancipation Proclamation had altered the course of the war. It was a calculated political move by Lincoln, designed as a last ditch effort to change the nature of the struggle to preserve the Union from a defensive one to an offensive one. He had said he would save the Union the shortest way under the Constitution, whether it be by freeing all the slaves, part of them, or none of them. Lincoln had wanted a crushing victory before issuing the document.

He had waited a year and a half for it, trying first one general and then another. When Lee withdrew from Maryland, the President had no alternative but to interpret this as the opportunity he needed for his famous Proclamation. If McClellan could not or would not convert Antietam into the necessary advantage, Lincoln must.

Those early September days did not foretell of the momentous events which would follow. To the military mind of Robert E. Lee there were clear-cut advantages in invading the North. Despite warning signals from several sources, he gambled the very existence of his army on gaining another victory over the Federal army. It seems obvious now, with the benefit of historical records, that the invasion was doomed to failure before it was launched.

The Army of Northern Virginia was in no condition to undertake such a monstrous task. There can be little doubt about the spirit of the Confederate soldier, but physically, Lee's army was exhausted. As he miscalculated the recuperative powers of the Federals, Lee also misjudged the capabilities of his own men and put them under an extravagant strain that all but diminished their strength and caused irreparable damage. How plain and simple fortitude replaced their inadequacies on the battlefield and during the weeks that followed Antietam is one of those marvelous chapters of history to which all Americans can point with pride.

Lee was not ignorant of his deficiencies. He wrote Jefferson Davis about them numerous times. So great was his confidence that with the exception of the night of September 14, when he had considered the possibility of withdrawal into Virginia, he did not once feel he would fail in Maryland. His miscalculations, however, were not intentional. If Lee ever believed he could beat the Federal army, he did so in September 1862.

This very belief led him across the river, guided the daring Special Orders No. 191, and finally, in the waning hours of the campaign, directed his stand at Sharpsburg. Though he confidently thought the consequences would be in his favor, in each of his decisions there was little hope, relatively little to gain, and so very much to lose. Though Lee was successful in capturing Harper's Ferry and its prize of prisoners and equipment, he did so at extreme risk. Lee was never taught at West Point to divide his army in the face of the enemy. "He practiced his own theory of the art of war," one military historian has written. "Although indebted to Napoleon, he treated each problem as a concrete case, which he solved according to circumstances, and he had his greatest success when he departed furthest from established rules."

The army was split with full knowledge that McClellan was approaching. Then McClellan found a copy of the plans and came uncomfortably close to putting a premature end to the campaign. Historian Douglas Southall Freeman, commenting on the results of the battle, said that it was not that "Lee was reckless but that McClellan was lucky." McClellan found fortune beyond compare in war, but because McClellan was McClellan, his luck at Antietam was minimized and Lee's fortune was enhanced. Lee made the best of the many advantages offered him; McClellan tossed away every one Lee gave him.

The Army of the Potomac would be defeated under other commanders before it would at last find victory. The Army of Northern Virginia would see spirits surge and strength regained and would again come close to gaining all that the Confederacy sought. But never again quite so close as during the 16 days of crisis in September 1862.

Great Britain's Lord Russell and Lord Palmerston shelved their plans for intervention and recognition; the fall elections came and went and little Southern support was gained; the state of Maryland remained impassive to its Confederate neighbors; and Abraham Lincoln turned a stalemate on the battlefield into a victory for the North with his Emancipation Proclamation. Antietam was the end of McClellan. It was the forecast of disaster for the Confederacy. It was a turning point in American history.

And on the night of September 17, 1862, one lone Union soldier lay beneath the darkened sky, contemplating, trying to figure out just what the Battle of Antietam had really been all about. He wrote:

There was no tree over our heads to shut out the stars, and as I lay looking up at these orbs moving so calmly on their appointed way, I felt, as never so strongly before, how utterly absurd in the face of high Heaven is this whole game of war, relieved only from contempt and ridicule by its tragic accompaniments, and by the sublime illustrations of man's nobler qualities incidentally called forth in its service. Sent to occupy this little planet, one among ten thousand worlds revolving through infinite space, how worse than foolish these mighty efforts to make our tenancy unhappy or to drive each other out of it.

McClellan
at Antietam

by Stephen W. Sears

ANTIETAM WAS THE ONLY BATTLE George McClellan ever directed from start to finish, and on it rests in large measure his reputation as a battlefield commander and tactician. McClellan's generalship on that bloody day may be examined by focusing on five issues:

(1) his picture of the enemy

(2) his appraisal of his own army and its generals

(3) his plan of battle for September 17

(4) the key decisions he made that day

(5) his refusal to renew the battle on September 18

It is important to examine first his view of the enemy, because that is the single most important element in any analysis of McClellan as a commander.

Within ten days of arriving in Washington in late July of 1861, he was persuaded that he was hugely outnumbered by the Confederates. He reached that conclusion on his own. It was only later "confirmed" by detective Allan Pinkerton, his director of military intelligence whose influence prevailed up to the eve of the Maryland Campaign in September of 1862.

In McClellan's mind, there was never a day or an hour when the Rebel army led by Generals Joe Johnston and P. G. T. Beauregard, and then by General Lee, numbered less than 100,000 men; usually the estimated number was far larger.

With the benefit of hindsight, and the Confederate returns, we know this was a great delusion. It was McClellan who always had the advantage in manpower, sometimes an overwhelming advantage. It is difficult to credit his delusion, and it has been suggested that he did not really believe these figures, but only used them as an excuse for his delays and failures and to gain reinforcements. He did indeed employ such excuses, but not out of subterfuge. His delusion was (so to speak) very real to him, and it was self-inflicted.

Only when his picture of the enemy is accepted do his actions throughout his career as head of the Army of the Potomac make sense. They are what any competent—if perhaps over-prudent—general would do when heavily outnumbered. To assume otherwise is to mark him down as stupid, and whatever else George McClellan may have been, he was not stupid.

The reasons McClellan could be thus deceived go deep into his character and extend well into his background. The Pinkerton reports reveal a pyramiding of error that finally produced monumental error. In the

Maryland Campaign, however, there was finally a chance for a clean sweep of the intelligence slate, for Pinkerton played no role in the fast-developing campaign.

Instead, when McClellan's dispatches to Washington are compared with the numerous intelligence reports in the Army of the Potomac's files, it is clear that in Maryland he relied almost entirely on cavalry to fill in his picture of the enemy.

As Jeb Stuart demonstrated, Civil War cavalry could be highly effective in gathering intelligence. But McClellan's cavalry commander, Alfred Pleasonton, was no Jeb Stuart, and his patrols never broke through Stuart's cavalry screen for a look at the Army of Northern Virginia. To be sure, plenty of Maryland civilians were eager to help, and there were Confederate stragglers and prisoners enough to keep Pleasonton busy interrogating them day and night, but he evaluated all this with a blind eye.

These country folk had never before seen so many men at one time, and they wildly exaggerated their numbers. Their stories were also highly colored by the trail of deceptions left by Stuart and Stonewall Jackson. Finally, those Rebels who were captured proved to be expert liars. A shrewd civilian in Frederick remarked that the favorite game among Lee's soldiers was bragging, "and they do it well."

Pleasonton was less perceptive. Ironically, he shared Allan Pinkerton's characteristic for great industry coupled with small judgment. He insisted on crediting Jackson with at least 80,000 men and James Longstreet with at least 30,000, and McClellan, to be on the safe side, announced to Washington that the "gigantic rebel army" facing him was 120,000 strong.

He expected nothing less, for George McClellan was a man of exceedingly stubborn convictions. He had long since decided that Robert E. Lee never dared meet him unless it was with a superior force, and certainly in this invasion of the North he would attempt nothing less. Consequently, McClellan counted three Confederate soldiers for every one actually facing him.

His judgments about his own troops, and especially about his generals, had much to do with his plan of battle and his decisions during the fighting on September 17. In the matter of their respective subordinates, Lee possessed an enormous advantage. His lieutenants were battle-proven and he had full confidence in them, particularly in his two corps commanders, Jackson and Longstreet.

Nor was his confidence misplaced. An Army of Northern Virginia historian, William Allan, had good cause to write that at Antietam the conduct of Lee "and his principal subordinates seems absolutely above criticism." By contrast, Antietam was badly fought on the Union side by several general officers, beginning with, it must be said, the general commanding.

Of his six corps commanders, McClellan had expressed full confidence in only two, Joe Hooker and Fitz John Porter. His old friend Ambrose Burnside was under censure for fumbling the pursuit of the Rebels after South Mountain (or so he was told by Porter, who nursed a grudge against Burnside stemming from the Second Manassas campaign). He had marked down another old friend, William Franklin, as slow and lacking in energy during the Peninsula Campaign.

On the Peninsula, too, he termed 65-year-old Edwin Sumner "even a greater fool than I had supposed," and blamed him for nearly losing a battle, and since then had done his best to keep Sumner from making command decisions. The sixth of the corps commanders, Joseph Mansfield, in his first combat assignment, was an unknown quantity and had been on the job only since September 15.

The troops of both Hooker and Mansfield were refugees from John Pope's luckless Army of Virginia, and were viewed by McClellan with mistrust. He put Hooker in charge of the I Corps, he wrote, to "make them fight if anyone can." McClellan always regarded the Army of the Potomac possessively as "his" army and "his" creation, yet during the Maryland Campaign more than half its troops were strangers to him. Only seven of the sixteen divisions at Antietam on September 17 had served under him in the field before.

Appraising McClellan's Antietam battle plan is complicated by the fact that he issued no written orders and called no conference of his corps commanders to present his ideas or explain them. As determined from their reports, he only communicated with his generals on a "need to know" basis, with the exception of Fitz John Porter. Porter seldom left his side, and may be considered his advisor and unofficial second in command.

Thus it is necessary to review McClellan's various explanations of what he termed his "design" for the battle—explanations that began to change with the passage of time and in response to criticism of his conduct of the fighting.

GEORGE B. MCCLELLAN BEGAN to shape his battle plan on his arrival before Sharpsburg on the afternoon of September 15. "My first rapid survey of the enemy's position inclined me to attack his left," he wrote in a draft of his memoirs. In the midst of the battle itself, he telegraphed Washington, "I have thrown the mass of the Army on their left flank. Burnside is now attacking their right," adding that his "small reserve" of Porter's corps was ready to attack the center "as soon as the flank movements are developed."

In his preliminary report on Antietam, written a month later, he referred again to his intention of making the main attack against the enemy left—the part of the battlefield north of the Dunker Church—and "at least to create a diversion in favor of the main attack" against the enemy right, exploiting any success with an assault on the center. On September 16 an aide heard him use the metaphor of pinching Lee in a vise.

From this evidence there can be little doubt that as he conceived it that day, it was McClellan's idea for Ambrose Burnside's IX Corps to make a diversion against Lee's right to prevent him from reinforcing his left where the main Union assault was to fall. He would seek to win the battle on the northern part of the field, where he judged the terrain best for maneuver, and said he was willing to stake two-thirds of his army to do so. That was clearly the understanding of both Burnside and his subordinate

Jacob Cox, expressed before the issue became a matter of controversy.

There is a theory that in fact McClellan's design was exactly the opposite: to draw Lee to the north so that Burnside might turn his right flank and cut his line of retreat to the Potomac and Virginia. But McClellan never wrote or said or claimed anything at the time that supports such a theory. As the battle progressed, this of course became a very real possibility, yet McClellan did not plan it that way and in any case he had by then so lost control of events that he was incapable of exploiting the opportunity.

Later, writing his report of his tenure as the commander of the Army of the Potomac, which was published in 1864, and working on his memoirs, published posthumously in 1887, McClellan recalled his plan for Antietam differently. The word "diversion" disappears in regard to the IX Corps, and Burnside's role (and subsequent failure) is magnified. But then in later years George McClellan recalled a good deal about his military career differently. He nursed many grievances in the wake of his removal from command in November 1862, and given time to reflect, he polished the record, shifted the blame, and settled old scores.

McClellan assigned his two most trusted lieutenants, Hooker and Porter, to the key roles in his design. Hooker's I Corps was to open the attack on the enemy left, while Porter with his V Corps would head the reserve, either to add the finishing touches to a victory or to anchor the final defense in case of defeat or retreat.

Hooker's assignment left Ambrose Burnside in high dudgeon. Having commanded both the I and IX Corps on the march into Maryland and at Turner's Gap, Burnside now found Hooker in an independent command at the opposite end of the battlefield and took it as a humiliation. In effect, the IX Corps now had two heads, the sulking Burnside, its former commander, and Jacob Cox, its current commander. It was an awkward situation, and in part because of it neither man would display initiative in the next day's battle.

McClellan's instructions to Hooker were verbal, and (according to Hooker) gave him the latitude to call for reinforcements from other commands and put them into action under his direction. After crossing Antietam Creek on the afternoon of September 16 to take up position for the attack, he quickly called on McClellan for support lest, as he put it, the enemy "eat me up." McClellan gave him Mansfield's XII Corps, almost certainly a deliberate attempt to solve the problem of handling Edwin Sumner.

Like Burnside, Sumner had commanded two corps in the opening phases of the campaign, his own II and Mansfield's XII Corps. By now taking the XII Corps from him and putting it at Hooker's call, McClellan reduced Sumner's control from one-third of the army to a single corps—albeit the largest and arguably the best in the Potomac army. Sumner, as his son and aide recalled, was preparing to lead the II Corps across the Antietam on the night of the 16th so as to retain the integrity of his two-corps command (and to add major support to the flank attack) when McClellan told him to remain east of the creek. He was to wait for further orders in the morning.

Once he had decided to bring Lee to battle on September 17, McClellan was slow to gather his own forces for the contest. Orders for Franklin's VI Corps in Pleasant Valley to join the main army were not sent until the evening of September 16, and Franklin did not start for the battlefield until the next morning. Even then, he marched with only two of his three divisions.

The division of Darius Couch set off that morning on McClellan's orders for Maryland Heights, a mission never satisfactorily explained; during the fighting on the 17th the order was countermanded. Nor did McClellan call for the last of his forces, Andrew Humphreys' division of the V Corps, then at Frederick, until the battle was underway.

As a consequence of these delayed decisions, the Army of the Potomac opened the Battle of Antietam short four of its divisions, or almost 23,000 effectives. Half of these men did not reach the field at all on the 17th, thanks to McClellan's tardy orders and (in the case of Couch's division) unaggressive leadership. The initial shock of battle was scheduled to be borne by John Pope's former troops, whom McClellan had characterized as "in bad condition as to discipline & everything else."

The diversion that was supposed to ease their way would be made by Burnside's IX Corps, which had seen its first hard fighting at South Mountain, led by a general in whom McClellan had little confidence. The troops McClellan classed as his best, the Peninsula veterans of the II, V, and VI corps, plus the cavalry massed as a reserve, were counted on to win the battle if it could be won, or to save the army if the enemy took control of events.

Because of his warped view of Lee's strength, McClellan fought the Battle of Antietam less to win than to prevent his own defeat. His attitude was expressed perfectly in the dispatch he sent to General-in-Chief Henry W. Halleck in Washington as the battle raged. After describing the fighting as the worst of the war, and perhaps of history, he wrote, "It will be either a great defeat or a most glorious victory." Although he subsequently decided this was too pessimistic a forecast to send to Washington and crossed out the sentence, concluding simply that he hoped God would grant him a glorious victory, the prospect of "a great defeat" dominated every decision he made on September 17.

McClellan would testify to the Joint Congressional Committee on the Conduct of the War that the Confederates were 100,000 strong on the Antietam battlefield, and his generals were of a like mind about the difficult odds they faced. Sumner told the committee that he calculated enemy strength at 80,000. Hooker thought that Lee took his stand at Sharpsburg with 50,000, later reinforced by Jackson from Harper's Ferry. Porter's chief of staff, certainly reflecting his superior's view, wrote that the enemy's strength that day was between 100,000 and 130,000. The fear of counterattack and ambush thus preoccupied McClellan and his key lieutenants throughout the daylong struggle.

Whether it was McClellan's or Hooker's decision to open the attack with the I Corps alone is not known—at least McClellan raised no objection—but the consequence was to blunt the thrust of the whole flanking operation. No attempt was made to broaden the front of the attack so as to overlap Nicodemus Heights to the west, from which Jeb

Stuart's artillery continued to pour a killing fire into the Federal columns. This could have been effected by using units of all three of the I Corps' divisions in the initial assault and bringing up the XII Corps in close support.

Hooker instead attacked with the divisions of Ricketts and Doubleday, holding Meade's division as his reserve and leaving Mansfield's corps to mark time a mile or so in the rear, presumably as a guard against a counterstrike by Lee's phantom divisions. Nicodemus Heights was the key piece of terrain on this part of the battlefield, and had Hooker seized it his artillery would have commanded the whole area between the Potomac River and the Hagerstown Pike—and enfiladed Jackson's position as well. If this ever occurred to McClellan, he left no record of it.

By the time the XII Corps was finally called to the rescue by Hooker, the I Corps had been struggling without support for an hour and a half and was shattered as an effective force. And when it did advance, the XII Corps found so many crises that it ended up being scattered across three-quarters of a mile or more and was nearly impossible to direct in any unified way.

These two Federal corps did some of the hardest fighting of the day under some of the best Federal leadership at the divisional and brigade levels. Yet by going into action "in driblets" (in Sumner's apt phrase) under the influence of McClellan's excessive caution, both were put out of action offensively, and the Confederate left, although severely battered, remained unbroken.

In retrospect, it can be seen that McClellan's mishandling of the II Corps was the fatal blow to his grand design for the battle. The benefits of hindsight are necessary, however, to see his actions as those of a general virtually obsessed by caution. No battle ever goes entirely according to plan, to be sure, but at Antietam General McClellan's overwhelming fear of defeat doomed his plan almost from the beginning.

Edwin Sumner, commander of the II Corps, was a man of simple thought patterns and no subtlety, and once the general commanding decided to launch his main attack on the enemy's flank, Sumner believed it ought to be a full-blooded attack. He was ready to do his part. Before six o'clock that morning he had his three divisions—15,200 fighting men, nearly as many as in the I and XII corps combined—ready to march, and was at McClellan's field headquarters at the Pry house for orders. By his aides' testimonies, McClellan refused to see him, and Sumner sat on the porch or paced impatiently while Hooker's battle raged.

McClellan did nothing until the crisis brought on by John Bell Hood's counterattack. Even then, had he previously advanced Sumner to a position somewhere near the battlefield, the intervention might have been decisive. There was shelter enough from Confederate artillery behind the East Woods, for example. Yet McClellan continued to hoard the entire II Corps defensively behind the Antietam, more than two miles from the fighting, until he decided what to do with it.

The combat integrity of the corps was immediately weakened by his decision to hold back Israel Richardson's division, for no better reason (so far as is known) than his concern that the unit supposed to take its place in the tactical reserve, George Morell's division of the V Corps, was camped a mile to the rear.

McClellan's thinking on this point is incomprehensible. Morell, for reasons equally obscure, required ninety minutes to move one mile. Meanwhile, Sumner had moved the divisions of John Sedgwick and William H. French forward without delay, but still it was nine o'clock before he reached the East Woods and was ready to attack. Here the chances of war took a hand in the matter, and the near destruction of John Sedgwick's division was the result.

Joe Hooker's wounding meant not only that Sumner went into action independently instead of under Hooker's direction—a circumstance McClellan most assuredly had not wanted—but also with a faulty conception of the situation. Sumner formed his own view with little regard for the facts, and without waiting for French led Sedgwick's troops personally in an attempt to turn Jackson's flank in the West Woods, and was in turn hit from the flank and driven from the field.

French, who had lagged behind on the march from the Antietam, now found himself alone and puzzled on the battlefield. Colonel Ezra Carman, who led the 13th New Jersey at Antietam and whose tactical study of the battle is definitive, wrote, "In the absence of orders for 'proper direction,' or for a movement in any direction, he came to the quick and proper conclusion to advance and form on the left of the troops he saw in position"—George Greene's division of the XII Corps—"and engage the Confederates in the Sunken Road...." Richardson, when finally released to go into action, had to go to French's aid. So the battle took a new direction, entirely without orders or direction from army headquarters.

McClellan made yet another decision that morning dictated by his exaggerated view of the Army of Northern Virginia. From his later efforts to change the record to make it appear that he issued his attack orders for Burnside's IX Corps as early as 8 a.m., it is clear enough that he hoped Burnside could prevent Lee from reinforcing his hard-pressed left. He actually gave the order only at 9:10 a.m.—the original order was found and published after McClellan's death—and he pegged it directly to the arrival of Franklin's VI Corps from Pleasant Valley to replenish the tactical reserve. As was the case with Richardson's division, McClellan would make no offensive commitment without an equal commitment to defense.

By about ten o'clock in the morning, after he learned the extent of Sumner's defeat, McClellan surrendered the initiative. As they arrived, Franklin's two divisions were sent to the right as defensive backing for Sumner. Two of Porter's brigades had the same mission. Battery after battery was put in line on the right, in anticipation of a counterstroke by the enemy.

When Israel Richardson, sensing a breakthrough at the Sunken Road, called for rifled guns to support a renewed attack and to suppress the Southern artillery (which was about all that remained of Lee's center), all that could be spared him from the Federal artillery array was one battery of smoothbores, too short-ranged for the job. Then Richardson was wounded and hard-fighting Winfield Scott Hancock put in his place.

Hancock was the ideal man to exploit the opportunity before him, but McClellan's orders to him were simply to hold his ground. These events did not reach McClellan second-hand. The entire fight for the Sunken Road took place under his watching eye; it was the only part of the Battle of Antietam he saw clearly from his field headquarters at the Pry house.

Meanwhile, his calls on Burnside to press his offensive and open a new front south of Sharpsburg grew increasingly strident. An aide heard him say to a courier, "Tell him if it costs 10,000 men he must go on now." Yet he continued to see Burnside's role as diversionary rather than decisive. He promised him support from the V Corps once he crossed the Antietam, but then reneged on the promise.

Cavalry commander Alfred Pleasonton, who had crossed the creek at the Middle Bridge and detected the near collapse of Lee's right flank, sent back a call for an immediate advance by the V Corps. He was turned down. The enemy was too strong, Porter told him, and he must "exercise caution." Pleasonton wrote in his report, "Decisive victory which was then within our grasp was lost to us by this inaction & apathy." (Before he submitted Pleasonton's report to Washington, McClellan deleted that part of it.)*

On the right, too, Franklin sent back a call for a renewed offensive, led by his two fresh divisions. McClellan

---

* Elements of George Sykes' division of Porter's V Corps did cross the Middle Bridge, and advanced a short distance along the Boonsboro Pike, but not in full concert with, or materially in support of, Burnside's advance.

took hope and rode to the front (the only time he did so that day) to see for himself. There is abundant eyewitness testimony that by now Sumner was thoroughly demoralized. He had been in the midst of Sedgwick's rout in the West Woods and it had been too much for him. He told two of McClellan's aides that he had all he could do just to hold his ground, although he was determined to do that. "Sir, tell the General I will *try* and hold my position—tell him, sir, I *will* hold it, I *will* hold it sir," one of them remembered him saying.

He was totally pessimistic when McClellan questioned him, and opposed any advance. In the face of similar pessimism from Burnside—when he at last won the bridge that bears his name, Burnside reported he *thought* he could hold it—McClellan sent orders to relieve him of his command if he did not advance. There was a considerably stronger case for Sumner to be relieved, yet McClellan left him in command, bowed to his wishes, and canceled any further offensive.

The last act of the Antietam drama, A. P. Hill's surprise attack on Burnside that ended the last Federal hope for a decisive victory on September 17, was the consequence of one of McClellan's most grievous failures that day. Whatever other use may be made of it, a basic purpose of cavalry is to guard against surprise. It is an oddity that the one-time captain of the 1st Cavalry, the author of a cavalry manual, and the inventor credited with the famous McClellan saddle, should have handled his cavalry so poorly when he became army commander.

Possibly it was because he never actually served in the field with the 1st Cavalry and took most of what he knew from books. Even so, posting cavalry on an army's flanks is such a fundamental precaution that McClellan's failure to do so at Antietam is genuinely perplexing. Perhaps the explanation lies in the fact that as early as the night of September 15, while Lee was bluffing him at Sharpsburg with some 15,000 men, McClellan concluded that the entire Confederate army was before him, united once more. Therefore, with no one to watch out for, he massed Pleasonton's troopers alongside Porter in the reserve in the hope of ordering a Napoleonic cavalry charge.

Thus Hill and most of his Light Division marched undetected from Harper's Ferry and wrecked Burnside's offensive. This clash produced McClellan's final decision of the day, and in view of the pattern of those decisions, it comes as no real surprise. Burnside called for help, McClellan promised him a battery, and said, "I can do nothing more. I have no infantry."

This of course was merely a figure of speech: a third of his infantry had yet to fire a shot on this terrible day. Burnside had to fall back to his bridge, but McClellan was satisfied. He had not been defeated by the Confederate host. He credited this in part to the fact that he had kept his reserves in place and so discouraged the enemy from attacking.

For all his days, George McClellan regarded Antietam as a great victory, the climax of his career. His boast to his wife on September 18—"Those in whose judgment I rely tell me that I fought the battle splendidly & that it was a masterpiece of art"—is a pathetic example of his self-deception, yet it was something he truly believed. Seen through his eyes, fending off defeat by an army larger than his own was indeed a masterpiece of art. And when Lee afterward crossed the Potomac back into Virginia, McClellan's pride soared. He had delivered Maryland and Pennsylvania from the invading horde.

For the Union the ultimate tragedy of Antietam is what might have been. Normally such speculation has no place in historical accounts, but Antietam is a special case. It was rare that a pitched battle in the Civil War ended in complete victory for one side or the other. (John Bell Hood's crushing defeat by George H. Thomas at Nashville in 1864 is an exception.) The fearful battle casualties exhausted winner as well as loser, the path of retreat was nearly always open, and (later in the war) entrenchments were too formidable to permit battles of annihilation. At Antietam, however, the ingredients for a total defeat of the Army of Northern Virginia were present, as they would not be again until Lee faced a like fate at Appomattox.

At Sharpsburg, Lee's army was far smaller than it had ever been before or would ever be again, until those last few days in April 1865. The usually accepted ratio of attackers over defenders counted for less on this field. Except for the defenders of the Sunken Road and Burnside Bridge, September 17 was for the most part a stand-up, slug-it-out combat, with opposing battle lines facing each other at almost point-blank range. In the charge and countercharge on the northern part of the field, for example, it was hard to classify who was on offense and who on defense, and the roughly equal casualties reflect that fact.

Further, Lee had no open line of retreat should any of the Federal near-breakthroughs—on Jackson's flank, or at the Sunken Road, or south of Sharpsburg where Burnside came so close to victory—have occurred under the driving leadership of a better commanding general. It is a common military axiom that a retreating army will outdistance a pursuing army, but not if the defeated army has a river at its back.

When it is considered how narrowly Lee escaped disaster three times that day, even with one out of three Yankee soldiers not engaged, it is reasonable to assume that something very close to a battle of annihilation could have taken place on the banks of the Potomac on September 17, 1862.

The same arguments for what "might have been" apply to September 18—"fatal Thursday," as a newspaper put it. Almost certainly in McClellan's place, a U. S. Grant (or a Robert E. Lee) would have renewed the battle that day. By the same token, it is all but impossible to imagine a general so consumed by self-deception as George McClellan doing so. He would claim he planned to fight again on September 19, but he made no plans and issued no orders to launch such an attack. It is permissible to speculate that he was perfectly satisfied to see Lee depart unmolested on the night of September 18. By his calculation McClellan had saved his army and his country, and that was honor enough for him.

McClellan committed any number of fundamental errors on the field of Antietam, many of them violations of what Francis Palfrey termed "the established principles of the military art." Perhaps the most fundamental error, and one that marks the entire course of his command of the Army of the Potomac, was to underestimate the fighting power of his own men. The judgment of Thomas Hyde, a Federal officer who fought at Antietam, is often quoted on this point, but it bears repeating. "It always seemed to me," Hyde wrote, "that McClellan, though no commander ever had the love of his soldiers more, or tried more to spare their lives, never realized the mettle that was in his grand Army of the Potomac. . . . He never appreciated until too late what manner of people he had with him."

ABOUT THE AUTHOR: STEPHEN W. SEARS, a former book editor at American Heritage, is the author of *Landscape Turned Red: The Battle of Antietam, George B. McClellan: The Young Napoleon,* and numerous other books and articles on the war.

Lincoln and McClellan meeting in the General's tent on the Antietam battlefield, October 4, 1862.

MAP 17
Tour Map
Antietam Battlefield
Part II

Refer also to the Tour Map on Pp. 44-45

A. P. Hill

Potomac River

C&O Canal

Ferry Hill Place

SHEPHERDSTOWN RD
(MD Rt 34)

⑦

MARYLAND

CANAL RD

SHEPHERDSTOWN

James Rumsey
Monument

⑧

Boteler's Ford

WEST
VIRGINIA

▲
N

1 mile

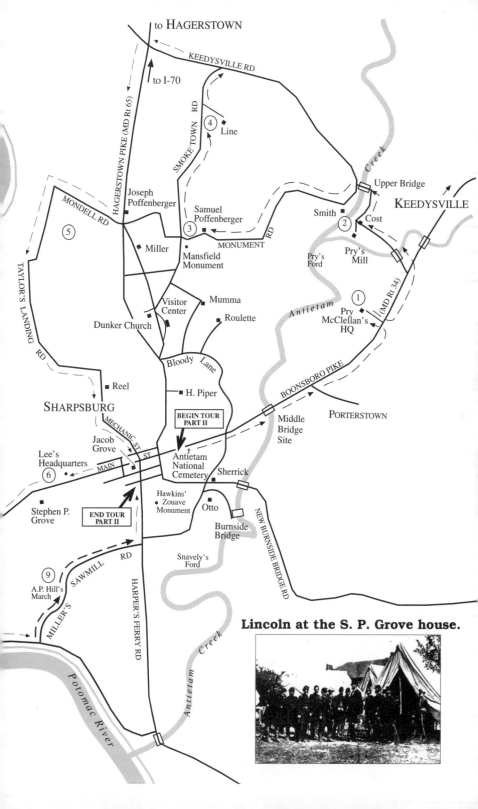

Lincoln at the S. P. Grove house.

The Battle of Antietam

Driving Tour of Part II Begins Here

Part I of the Antietam Tour ended at the Antietam National Cemetery. Part II, comprehending the outlying areas of the battlefield, proceeds from the cemetery northeast along the Boonsboro Pike (Maryland Rt. 34).

IMPORTANT NOTE: Many of the sites in Part II are privately owned. Please respect the privacy of the owners and do not trespass.

1. PHILIP PRY HOUSE—McCLELLAN'S HQ

1.0 mile beyond the National Cemetery, Md. Rt. 34 crosses Antietam Creek at the approximate location of the wartime Middle Bridge (sometimes called the Antietam Bridge). Unlike the Lower (Burnside) Bridge and Upper Bridge, the structure here is not the original; it was destroyed by a flood in 1891 after standing for almost a century. The Middle Bridge area marks the approximate center of McClellan's line. Here much of the artillery, and virtually all of the cavalry, were massed.

2.0 miles from the cemetery (and 1.0 mile past the Middle Bridge) is a small blue and gray marker on the right side of the road indicating a turn to the left (west) to the Pry house. A tree-lined gravel road, which retains much of its rustic, wartime appearance, leads a short distance back to the house.

Philip Pry, his wife Elizabeth Ellen Cost, and five children, Samuel (14), Alfred (11), Jacob (5), Charles (3) and Anna (1), lived here in 1862 making a living farming their surrounding 125 acres. The high ground where the Prys' brick, 2-story house is situated, overlooks Antietam Creek from the east bank. In 1862 the ground offered a panoramic view of the farms and fields stretching across the Antietam Valley to the west, particularly the Mumma and Roulette farms, and the Sunken Road leading to the Newcomer farm which became known as Bloody Lane. (Much of this wartime vista has been obstructed by vegetation.)

It was this location that McClellan selected as his headquarters, and on the morning of the battle the Pry family, at McClellan's direction, was relocated to Keedysville for safety. The one failure of the Pry house as a point of observation was that both flanks of the army, where the principal operations against Lee's line were to be conducted, were concealed from view. McClellan spent most of the battle here, sometimes viewing the fighting from a trapdoor in the roof. He ventured over to the west side of the creek only once during the battle, some time after 2 p.m., to confer with Sumner and Franklin on the northern sector of the field, and thereupon concluded that his right was in no shape to launch further attacks.

Before the Pry family's brush with history was over, many Federal officers paid a visit to their farm. It is reported that Captain George A. Custer was one of the first officers to arrive at the Pry home, to apprise them of McClellan's desire to locate his headquarters there. General Fitz John Porter was Little Mac's constant companion and confidant at headquarters while the battle raged.

Philip Pry House

General Edwin V. Sumner arrived at this house on the morning of the battle, impatiently seeking orders to advance his huge II Corps, but was left pacing as McClellan analyzed and deliberated the battle unfolding out of view to his far right. After Joe Hooker's wounding (a bullet in the foot while riding toward the front near the Dunker Church), he was brought to the Pry house for treatment.

Another officer, the mortally wounded General Israel B. "Fighting Dick" Richardson, was brought here. He was one of the best Union commanders on the field at Antietam. Had McClellan properly supported him with artillery during the Bloody Lane fighting—which occurred right under Little Mac's nose from his vantage point at the Pry house—Richardson might very well have broken the Confederate center. A row of guns was little more than a mile from the Sunken Road, serving no real purpose at the time, but Richardson was forced to fight with only one battery of short-range smoothbores against an impressive array of Rebel artillery.

Richardson had just spoken with his sole battery, instructing them to prepare to advance, when he was struck down by Confederate guns. "Fighting Dick," who had earned the respect and admiration of his division as well as President Lincoln (the President paid him a visit at the Pry house during his October meeting with McClellan), died of his wounds November 3, 1862, in a second floor bedroom of the Pry home.

By the time of Lincoln's visit McClellan had moved from the Pry house. After learning of Lee's retreat across the Potomac, on September 20 McClellan relocated his headquarters to the western edge of Sharpsburg, the

exact location never verified but probably in the neighborhood of the Stephen P. Grove farm, where his friend Porter
had established his base. On the 27th he moved again, to
another location which also remains a mystery, but which
several historians speculate was on the Reverend J.
Adams property on the east side of the Harper's Ferry
Road, at a point about three-quarters of a mile southwest
of Snavely's Ford.

The National Park Service now owns the Pry house,
and while the exterior can be inspected by visitors, the
house is not open to the public.*

2. SAMUEL PRY'S MILL/PRY'S FORD/UPPER BRIDGE

*After returning to the main road (Rt. 34), turn left, then proceed 0.6 mile
to the intersection with the Keedysville Road and turn left again. A short
distance beyond this turn the Keedysville Road crosses the Little
Antietam by a bridge which appears similar in construction to the other
Antietam bridges, but should not be confused with the Upper Bridge,
which is just over a half-mile ahead. Approximately 0.4 mile past the
Little Antietam crossing, the Keedysville Road makes a sharp turn to the
right; the side road to the left at this bend leads back to Pry's mill, a
stone's throw away. (The Upper Bridge, alternately known as Hitt's
Bridge—after Samuel Hitt, who was instrumental in its construction—
or Hooker's Bridge, is just around the bend in the Keedysville Road.) The
mill is private property.*

The large, brick structure here, located on the northern bank of the Little Antietam, was a gristmill operated

---

* Betty Otto of the NPS notes that the wartime exterior of the Pry house had a short porch,
or stoop, at the main entranceway, and that the long porch running the length of the front
of the house, pictured in some postwar views of the property, was a later addition. When
the porch was damaged by fire in recent years, the subsequent restoration included a short
porch to more closely match the house's wartime appearance. Betty also noted, regarding
the family, that Philip Pry was of German descent. The "old country" name was Bryne,
shortened to Bry in America, then was later changed to Pry.

by Samuel Pry, Philip's brother. Hooker's I Corps and Mansfield's XII Corps passed by this mill on their way to the northern sector of the battlefield, where the opening attacks took place. Hooker, who crossed the Antietam on the afternoon of the 16th, and Mansfield, who followed later that night, used the nearby Upper Bridge and adjacent shallows. The units that followed next day (Sumner's II Corps and two divisions of Franklin's VI Corps) utilized a shorter route by way of Pry's Ford, a shallow area extending several hundred yards and beginning approximately 100 yards below Antietam Creek's confluence with the Little Antietam (or some 500 yards below the Upper Bridge).*

Thus, the bulk of the men comprising the Army of the Potomac—some 50,000 of them—tramped through this general vicinity on their way to uncertain fates in Miller's cornfield, the West Woods, and Bloody Lane. Some 200 casualties from Hooker's and Mansfield's corps were treated at Pry's mill. A medical inspector reported on the treatment here: "Surgeons are young and often under stimulation [alcohol]. Management poor."

On the opposite side of the Keedysville Road is the Jacob Cost house. (Jacob was Elizabeth Pry's father.) The house served temporarily as I Corps division commander

---

* Pry's Ford has been indicated on wartime and modern maps at so many different points between the Upper Bridge and the large bend in Antietam Creek in rear of the Philip Pry house that confusion often results as to the exact crossing point. Of course, unlike a bridge, which occupies a specific location, a ford may constitute many shallow points along the bank depending on ever-changing water levels and the imagination of local property owners to select names for specific shallow points. Pry's Ford, for example, appears to be the general reference for the shallows beginning at a small island in the Antietam just below its confluence with the Little Antietam, and extending for some distance downstream. (The ford is no longer used and all the surrounding ground is private property.)

Pry's Mill

George G. Meade's headquarters. General Mansfield had his last meal here the evening of the 16th (he would die of wounds at Antietam); and, like nearly every farmhouse in the vicinity of Sharpsburg/Keedysville, it became a field hospital on the 17th.

3. SAMUEL POFFENBERGER FARM

After crossing the Antietam at the Upper Bridge make an abrupt left, leaving the Keedysville Road and taking the road south; the Samuel Poffenberger farm (now called the Kefauver-Poffenberger farm) is 1.6 miles away on the right side of the road. Along the way are many wartime structures, most of which were used as hospitals after the battle, in particular the O. J. Smith farm on the left, at the first wide turn past the Upper Bridge. The Samuel Poffenberger and O. J. Smith farms are private property.

For many years it was believed that Clara Barton— former school teacher, clerk in the U.S. Patent Office, and famous Civil War nurse—tended the wounded at Joseph Poffenberger's farm, north of Miller's cornfield and behind the North Woods. But more recent findings tend to indicate that Samuel's farmhouse was the scene of her heroic mission. While she undoubtedly visited many of the field hospitals, it was probably here at the Samuel Poffenberger farm that she arrived as the battle was still raging and assisted Dr. James Dunn of Pennsylvania. Wounded and dying already filled the house and covered the porch and adjacent grounds. More men with hideous wounds staggered in or were carried to the place as the battle continued in all its fury less than a mile away.

Clara had witnessed the bloody aftermath of other battles and knew well the needs of the wounded and those attending them. She brought with her bandages—which

Dr. Dunn sorely needed—medicine, food, lanterns, and other supplies, transported in a covered wagon loaned to her by the army. Four assistants accompanied her. While attending a wounded man a bullet passed under Clara's arm and killed the soldier who was accepting a drink from her.

After Antietam, where Clara Barton witnessed so much suffering and was so close to the fighting that she herself came under fire, her mission assumed greater proportions. With more wagons and supplies she could save more lives and she set out to obtain them from the army. Her requests granted, she soon was following the troops to other battlefields, and continued to do so throughout the war.

In 1865, only three months after Joe Johnston surrendered to William T. Sherman in North Carolina, rounding out the capitulation of the two principal Confederate armies, Clara Barton was at Andersonville Prison in Georgia, assisting an expedition marking the graves of almost 13,000 Union soldiers who died there.

The Samuel Poffenberger farm remained a field hospital after Clara and (apparently) Dr. Dunn moved on. A Dr. Chaddock and an assistant named Young, and a captured Confederate physician, continued the work of tending the wounded here. Unlike the condition at the Pry's mill hospital, the medical report on the Samuel Poffenberger farm states: "Faithfully managed, every patient properly and kindly treated. Success good. No ambulances. Dr. Chaddock has been overworked, has had but one assistant except a Confederate Surgeon, who has taken care of his patients very faithfully."

Clara Barton

Joseph K. F. Mansfield

Clara Barton's memorial is at the Joseph Poffenberger farm, even though it is now believed she spent most of her time at Samuel's farm. At right is the Mansfield Monument along the Smoketown Road where he fell.

The contrast in reports between the two hospitals brings to focus a point often ignored by those who might ponder losses in battle. But true enough, a wounded soldier's survival very often hung in a peculiar balance of medical competence and happenstance, depending on the quality of treatment accorded at the nearest field hospital.

4. GEORGE LINE HOUSE

Continue along the same road to its intersection with the Smoketown Road, where the monument to General Mansfield sits, and turn right. (The upturned cannon and monument indicate the approximate location where Mansfield fell mortally wounded.) About 0.1 mile away the paved road bends to the left and a dirt road continues straight. Take the dirt road. CHECK YOUR ODOMETER HERE. The George Line house is 1.2 miles away, set back from the road on the right side.

This stretch of the Smoketown Road is undeveloped and is one of the few original battlefield roads that still retains much of its wartime ambience. General George S. Greene's division of Mansfield's XII Corps followed this road to reach the battlefield. After his wounding, General Mansfield was carried out this road to the home of George Line. A driveway leads back to the Line house, a residence situated beyond some agricultural experimentation buildings. The house is somewhat difficult to notice because the blue and gray painted marker indicating the historic farmhouse faces the opposite direction of your approach. A good landmark to use is the large barn-like structure of the experimental complex. The Line house is private property.

The George Line house marks the vicinity of the XII Corps' camp on the eve of battle. The men had stumbled through the darkness to reach this spot after ordered by McClellan to support Hooker, who had crossed the Antietam by daylight earlier that afternoon (September 16). By most indications, General Alpheus Williams' division camped immediately behind the Line house, with George Greene's division camped just east of them.

Next morning, as the XII Corps maneuvered behind Hooker's left, men of Hood's Confederate division still occupied portions of the East Woods, through which the Smoketown Road passes. General Mansfield was at the front, personally directing his regiments into line, when he saw the 10th Maine firing into the woods nearby. Believing they were firing into Hooker's troops, Mansfield demanded that they cease their ill-directed fire.

The Maine men angrily protested that indeed they were Rebels, who had been firing at them from the moment of their arrival. Just then a line of gray showed itself and Mansfield had to concede, saying, "Yes, yes, you are right." At that moment, shots rang out and the general was hit in the chest, his horse also being injured in the volley. Mansfield managed to dismount himself, was placed in an ambulance, and carried back to the Line house where he suffered through the night and died next day.

General Joseph King Fenno Mansfield, a native of Connecticut, was three months short of his 59th birthday when he was struck down at Antietam. He had entered West Point at age 13, later graduating second in the class of 1822 after five years' training. He fought conspicuously in the Mexican War, and afterward, through the efforts of Secretary of War Jefferson Davis, obtained the rank of colonel on the Inspector General's staff. With the outbreak of the Civil War he was assigned to fortify Washington, D.C., a duty he pursued with vigor and telling effectiveness. But he yearned for a field command. He got his wish in the midst of Lee's first invasion of the North and joined the XII Corps as its commander on September 15, 1862, never before in charge of such a large body of troops.

At 58, Mansfield was the third oldest among all division, corps and army commanders in both armies at Antietam. (Only "Bull" Sumner at 65 and George S. Greene, 61, a division commander in the XII Corps, were his elders.) Mansfield's two-day stint in active field service during the Civil War was probably the high point of the old soldier's career. One can only imagine the thrilling anticipation that must have gripped the commander as he arose in the pre-dawn darkness of that crisp, foggy September morning, listening to the murmur of voices in camp and the rattling of equipment of the thousands of men under his command preparing for the big fight to come.

Many of the young men in Mansfield's command drew a certain measure of comfort and security seeing the white-haired officer at their head. In those two short days he had won over the men of the XII Corps who cheered him whenever he rode by. But Antietam would be his first and last battle in this war, and he was denied even seeing the glorious advance of his men in full battle array.

Mansfield's successor, General Alpheus Williams, referred to Mansfield in his official report of the battle as "the accomplished and distinguished commander of the corps." But, more privately, in a letter to his daughter written six days after the battle, Williams wrote: "Poor Gen. Mansfield, who took command of our corps two days before the battle, was an excellent gentleman, but a most fussy, obstinate officer. He was killed just as the head of our column reached the battlefield. . . ." This was just where one might expect a fussy, obstinate sort to be: at the front of his column, tending to the details. Mansfield, the only corps commander killed or mortally wounded at Antietam, is buried in Middletown, Connecticut.

5. NICODEMUS HEIGHTS (or HILL)

Continue along the Smoketown Road 0.2 mile to its intersection with the Keedysville Road and turn left, then left again on the Hagerstown Pike, 0.8 mile away. About 1.5 miles past this turn, take Mondell Road to the right, which climbs Nicodemus Heights. There are no interpretive markers here or designated pull-over areas, so to view the landscape use your own judgment, but even though it is a mere country road, be watchful of local traffic when stopping. The principal gun positions on the heights were off to the left (south) side of Mondell Road.

This rise, perhaps over-glorified by terming it "heights" or a "hill," was nevertheless a key position at Antietam, one that is usually overlooked by visitors. A large portion of Jeb Stuart's cavalry occupied this area, with the redoubtable Maj. John Pelham and his horse artillery posted here on the high ground. From this position the guns commanded the Hagerstown Pike and its surrounding fields and woodlots. It was also without doubt the key position in support of Jackson's left flank; Stonewall could not have held his position long with Yankee artillery on this ridge.

That fact seems to have escaped the notice of Joe Hooker, who ultimately sent his I Corps directly across the path of Pelham's guns and other batteries posted south of him along the ridge. An infantry detachment sent to dislodge the Confederates here, or a flanking operation for the same purpose by a formidable host of cavalry (which was inactive most of the day, massed at McClellan's center near the Middle Bridge), would have materially aided the Union's opening attacks, and might well have turned the tide had they wrestled their own guns to the position.

As it turned out, however, the Confederates exploited their advantages of position and nonmolestation and poured iron death into the flank of the advancing Yankees. As the battle tide moved farther south, the batteries simply moved to their right, following the action, many eventually taking position on Hauser Ridge, a southern extension of Nicodemus Heights. The repulse of the Union assault into the West Woods was partially due to the effectiveness of artillery on these ridges; Sedgwick's troops emerged from the west edge of the West Woods into the very muzzles of Confederate guns.

Later in the day, a flanking movement under the direction of Jeb Stuart, with the intended purpose of gaining the Union rear, was planned on the Confederate left. Twenty-one guns were moved to the far northern end of Nicodemus Heights in support of the plan, with seven regiments of cavalry and the 48th North Carolina infantry poised to deliver an attack. George Meade, however, now in command of the I Corps after Hooker's wounding, had guarded against such an event by placing nearly three dozen artillery pieces, massed wheel to wheel, facing west near the Joseph Poffenberger farm. The gun array was enough to make even the cavalier Stuart think twice, and the mission was abandoned.

As you look south along the ridge, the back slope and valley to your right is where the Confederates' limbers and caissons were concealed from enemy view and protected from their fire. Mobility of the guns was enhanced by the road—Taylor's Landing Road—running parallel to and behind the ridges, the same road on which the tour continues.

6. LEE'S HEADQUARTERS

Where Mondell Road intersects Taylor's Landing Road, turn left; this road runs behind the ridges and between them and the Potomac River, eventually intersecting with Main Street in Sharpsburg, some three miles away. Along the way, past the ninety degree bend near Sharpsburg, is the Reel farm, a battlefield landmark. At the intersection with Main Street, on the southwest corner, is a large brick house, formerly the home of Jacob H. Grove, where a conference was held between Lee and his principal officers on the evening of September 17. At this intersection turn right onto Main Street (Md. Rt. 34), and proceed 0.7 mile to where a monument set back from the road on the right marks Lee's headquarters site; a pull-over space on the shoulder is provided.

This patch of grass and shade marks the location of the small grove of trees where General Robert E. Lee pitched his headquarters tents at Sharpsburg. Unlike McClellan, whose headquarters was behind convex lines, Lee was fortunate to be behind a concave position where he could efficiently utilize the benefits of interior lines; this spot, where he made his headquarters, is at the approximate center of the position.

Monument at Robert E. Lee's headquarters site.

A short ride to the ridge on the opposite side of Main St. offered Lee a fine view of his right. And today, if you walk to the tree line behind the headquarters monument and peer through the trees, you can see across the meadows (foliage permitting) some of the tops of monuments in the West Woods barely a mile away, offering visual confirmation of the optimum position of Lee's base.

At dawn on the day of the Battle of Antietam, General Lafayette McLaws' division was camped in the fields behind Lee's headquarters, and later that morning marched off to the north to reinforce Jackson. Across the road (south) from Lee's headquarters was General Richard H. Anderson's division, which was handily dispatched to the assistance of D. H. Hill's division fighting at Bloody Lane.

7. FERRY HILL PLACE

Continue along Md. Rt. 34 for 2.4 miles to "Ferry Hill Place," on the right side of the road just before the Potomac River bridge; there are markers at the site. (The beautifully restored home is now headquarters for the C&O Canal division of the NPS and is not open to the public.) Along the way, on the left side of the road, set back several hundred yards from Rt. 34 and approximately 0.6 mile beyond Lee's HQ site, is the Stephen P. Grove house. The house was the headquarters of General Fitz John Porter and very possibly nearby was McClellan's second Sharpsburg headquarters site, though the latter's exact location still remains somewhat of a mystery. The large brick Grove house appears in the background of one of the famous Alexander Gardner photographs of Lincoln visiting V Corps headquarters.

One of the most famous and readable first-hand accounts of the Civil War, *I Rode With Stonewall*, came from the pen of Henry Kyd Douglas, staff officer with Stonewall Jackson, and later in field command with the rank of colonel in the last days of the war. In his oft-cited memoirs, Douglas makes several references to his home at "Ferry Hill Place" overlooking the Potomac. While the house is only incidental to the Antietam battle, its connection with Douglas alone makes it a worthwhile stop on the tour.

The opening paragraph of Douglas' book mentions Ferry Hill Place, and the next one tells how in 1859 old John Brown, then using the alias Isaac Smith to conceal his widespread reputation as a militant abolitionist, was struggling up from the Potomac bank near Ferry Hill Place with a heavily laden wagon. Douglas learned from the old man that he was hauling boxes of miner's tools, so he offered some assistance (his father's carriage horses) to help haul the load up the steep bank. Of course, a short time later John Brown raided the nearby Harper's Ferry arsenal, attempting to foment a slave uprising, and the true contents of the boxes of "miner's tools" became known: they were the "pikes" with which Brown intended to arm the slaves.

Early into Lee's Maryland Campaign, Douglas received permission to visit his father, mother and sister at Ferry Hill Place. After dark he made his way to Shepherdstown, crossed the Potomac at Boteler's Ford (the bridge had been destroyed earlier in the war), and made his way to his home for a brief stay, returning to camp by 3 a.m. Little did he know that the great invasion would reach a head only a few miles from his house.

After the Battle of Antietam and the retreat of Lee on the night of September 18, Ferry Hill Place fell into Union hands. In Douglas' telling: "Now in a night, as it were, a beautiful farm was laid waste, its fences disappeared up to the doors of the mansion house, artillery parks filled the

Ferry Hill Place. Inset is a photo of Henry Kyd Douglas, taken shortly after the war, with his Confederate uniform coat thrown over his shoulder.

wheat fields; corn and fodder and hay soon became contraband of war."

This description is typical of what happened any time an army, Union or Confederate, bivouacked in an area. Rail fences were the first victims, used for firewood, and generally whatever provisions that could be found were consumed. Artillery had to park somewhere, and best off the road so as not to impede other traffic. However, every army contains a certain share of ne'er-do-wells, profiteers and scoundrels, and at the hands of this undesirable element Ferry Hill Place was ransacked.

According to Douglas, the invaders plundered wardrobes and bureaus, speared mattresses with their bayonets and tossed them on the floor, and used "brutal language" to his family. Due to an alleged fluke circumstance, Douglas' father, Reverend Robert Henry Douglas, later came under suspicion as a spy and was jailed for six weeks. He was released on parole with the stipulation that he could not leave the grounds of Ferry Hill Place.

An incident of blue-gray fraternization occurred at Ferry Hill Place shortly after the Battle of Antietam, while Union troops still occupied the area. Douglas relates that he received permission from Stonewall Jackson to ride to Shepherdstown and at least look across the Potomac for signs of his family's fate under the conditions of a military occupation. While on the river bank he was hailed by a Union cavalry sergeant on the opposite side who invited him over for a visit. Reluctant at first, he was comforted by the sergeant who said that all the officers were at dinner in Sharpsburg, and that he would guarantee a safe return. A boat was sent over. Douglas was greeted on the other side by some fifty curious troopers who, when his identity was made known, asked every manner of question about his enigmatic mentor and their army's most tenacious adversary, Stonewall Jackson.

Douglas' mother was summoned to the river bank and the two had a brief reunion as Union soldiers stood a respectful distance away with uncovered heads. Afterward the sergeant promised that he would look after the family for him and, according to Douglas, "So far as I know the Sergeant was as good as his word . . . and while the company remained at 'Ferry Hill Place,' my father's family was never molested." (It was after this cavalry company was called away for other duty that Douglas' father was arrested as an alleged spy.)

A Jackson tale punctuates this story. After his safe return to camp, Douglas related the whole story to Stonewall who fumed at the risks taken. Douglas wrote that he shot back with, "General, I couldn't help it . . . Stonewall Jackson wouldn't have refused to see his mother under such circumstances," at which the general, in Douglas' words, was "routed." "He rose from his chair with some wild remark about a 'lame excuse,'" Douglas wrote, "but as he went into his tent I failed to discover the faintest trace of indignation or reproach lingering around the back of his neck."

During the Maryland Campaign, two notable Confederate officers were treated at Ferry Hill Place for injuries sustained in battle or on the march: Colonel W. H. F. "Rooney" Lee, the commander's son, who was hurt in a fall from his horse, and General Alexander Lawton, division commander under Jackson, was brought here after suffering wounds in the fighting around the Dunker Church.

NOTE: At the end of this Tour (Pg. 149) are listed two selected points of interest in Shepherdstown, WV, just across the river. If you desire to visit these sites it is convenient at this point to proceed over the bridge and do so, then return to this location to resume the Main Tour.

8. BOTELER'S FORD

From Ferry Hill Place take the Canal Road, which runs south off Md. Rt. 34 just opposite the pull-over area and markers. CHECK YOUR ODOM-ETER... The C & O Canal ditch runs parallel to the Potomac and the river side of Canal Road is mostly heavily wooded all along. Clearings and convenient canal ditch crossing points are few, so to be sure you find the right one, do a mileage count. The distance from Ferry Hill Place to the best vantage point to view Boteler's Ford is exactly 1.45 miles; when you near this count you'll see the pull-over area, the small clearing in the trees, and the worn path.

Boteler's Ford, alternately referred to as Blackford's Ford (and sometimes Pack Horse Ford or Shepherdstown Ford), was Lee's only link to Virginia—and virtually his only escape route should the tide go against him—as he made his stand at Sharpsburg; the Potomac River bridge had been burned in 1861. After Stonewall Jackson's capture of the Harper's Ferry garrison, he reached Sharpsburg by crossing at Boteler's, and on the afternoon of the 17th, A. P. Hill's men splashed across here after a forced march from Harper's Ferry to save Lee's right.*

To protect the ford, Lee had placed several batteries on the (West) Virginia side. They were also in position to support any hasty retreat—dare say, rout—that might ensue should McClellan press fully his advantages and attempt to cut-off the Confederates from their lifeline. One

---

* Lee with Longstreet's column had fallen back on Sharpsburg from the north after South Mountain, so did not reach the field by way of Boteler's Ford.

Boteler's Ford, viewed from the Maryland side of the Potomac River.

objective of Burnside's assault was to do just that, but the arrival of A. P. Hill's division foiled the plan. As Hill's footsore men stumbled up to Boteler's and began wading the Potomac, they undoubtedly passed some of the many wagon-loads of wounded coming from the opposite direction, headed for the hospitals established in Shepherdstown. But the grisly sight seems not to have lessened the Light Division's pace.

On the 18th, Lee issued orders for a retreat into Virginia. The long wagon train was the first to leave and was soon crossing at Boteler's Ford. Then that night, after the trains were safely across, the ragged survivors of the army began to filter away from the front and onto the roads to the ford. Torches lit the crossing point. The last troops to cross were those of General John G. Walker's division. Walker found Lee sitting on his horse in the river watching the steady procession of troops, wagons and artillery, and hailed the commander. "Returning my greeting," wrote Walker, "he inquired as to what was still behind. There was nothing but the wagons containing the wounded, and a battery of artillery, all of which were near at hand, and I told him so. 'Thank God!' I heard him say as I rode on."

With his crossing completed, Lee left General William N. Pendleton on the high ground along the river at Shepherdstown with ten batteries and some supporting infantry to thwart any pursuit by McClellan. Such a stab at Lee's rear was made the morning of the 19th by Alfred Pleasonton's cavalry, with Porter's V Corps coming along behind. An artillery duel fought across the river consumed several hours, and it appeared that Pendleton had the situation under control, until some stubborn bluecoats managed to reach the Shepherdstown bank. In a panic, Pendleton caught up with Lee and explained that his whole force, including all ten batteries (the reserve artillery), was lost to the enemy. Lee was markedly affected by the alarming news, and Jackson, determined to see that the loss was only temporary, ordered A. P. Hill's division to rush back to Boteler's Ford.

The Federal force that had crossed the river was only one Michigan regiment, which had been recalled later that night and camped in the canal towpath. As Hill's men approached Shepherdstown next morning, they met no resistance, so pushed on toward the ford where they discovered Porter's corps in the process of crossing. After a brief but sharp contest, the Federals were driven into the river and back to the Maryland bank, and the fight ended.

Hill, who seems to have greatly over-magnified the skirmish, called it a "most terrible slaughter" of the enemy and rejoiced that the Federals had lost "3000 killed and drowned." Porter, however, reported his losses at only a tenth that number, two-thirds of which were from the 118th Pennsylvania, a hapless regiment armed with inferior weapons and unable to defend themselves properly. Hill turned to rejoin the main body with the rear guard and artillery (less four guns) intact.

9. A. P. HILL'S MARCH (Miller's Sawmill Road)

Continue along Canal Road 0.8 mile to the intersection with Miller's Sawmill Road and turn left. The length of Miller's Sawmill Road, from the turn off of Canal Road to the intersection with the Harper's Ferry Road, is 1.7 miles, and follows the route of A. P. Hill's advance from Harper's Ferry on September 17, as the battle raged on Lee's right flank.

After A. P. Hill's Light Division crossed the Potomac at Boteler's Ford, his artillery placed in the van so as not to be slowed by the infantry, the whole force began its climb up the river bank toward Lee's imperiled right flank. The path of Hill's approach—as Burnside's assault, though tardy, was nevertheless threatening to cut-off the nearly fought-out Army of Northern Virginia from its only line of retreat—followed the course of the road leading away from Miller's sawmill, near the Potomac, and intersecting the main Maryland-side route to Harper's Ferry on the high ground. Hill, sporting his red battle shirt, seemed a man possessed that day. One report says that as he arrived on the battlefield he spied a lieutenant cowering behind a tree. The fiery general reined up near the officer, demanded his sword, broke it over the soldier's back, then rode off to spur his men onward.

Douglas Southall Freeman wrote of Hill and his march from Harper's Ferry: "The impetuosity that had been his vice was now his spur. . . . Every sound of fire was his summons. Speed the march, close up, close up! The life of the Confederacy might depend on the pace of that one Division." Bruce Catton described the march this way: "Hill drove his men so cruelly that he left fully half of his division panting along the roadside—but he got up those who were left in time to stave off disaster and keep the war going for two and one half more years."

Hill had started the Maryland Campaign under arrest as a result of one of his clashes with Stonewall and charges of insubordination and neglect of duty. He was forced to follow in rear of his command until the arrest order was suspended when battle loomed. A similar fate had befallen John Bell Hood (as mentioned in Part I of the

Tour), and both officers ultimately played critical roles in the Battle of Antietam.

At the Harper's Ferry Road intersection turn left. The view from along this road shows the field of Hill's counterattack. Continue into Sharpsburg. At the intersection with Main Street (Rt. 34), if you have not already done so, reconsider visiting the Points of Interest in Shepherdstown on the next page. Turn left on Rt. 34 to go to Shepherdstown, or right to reach Rt. 65 with connections to I-70.

This concludes the Tour of the Antietam Battlefield. Ask your local bookseller about other Blue & Gray Magazine History and Tour Guides to Civil War Battlefields, or call us direct at 1-800-CIVIL WAR.

Antietam National Cemetery

POINTS OF INTEREST IN SHEPHERDSTOWN, WV

To reach Shepherdstown, proceed southwest from Sharpsburg on Md. Rt. 34, past "Ferry Hill Place," and cross the Potomac at the James Rumsey Bridge. The road becomes W. Va. Rt. 480 in Shepherdstown. (This was Virginia in 1862. The state of West Virginia was formed in June 1863.)

JAMES RUMSEY MONUMENT—*east on W. Va. Rt. 230 in town, which is German St.; where 230 turns south, continue straight on German St., then left on Mill St., just before the RR tracks; proceed to the dead-end at the Potomac overlook.*

The monument honors James Rumsey, pioneer in steam navigation, who tested his steam-powered boat in the Potomac at Shepherdstown in the 1780s. The panoramic view of the Potomac River and Maryland shore offered from this point is why it is included as a point of interest. Looking slightly upstream, Ferry Hill Place can be seen sitting atop the opposite bluffs, very likely the same scene presented to Henry Kyd Douglas during his post-battle visit to his home. Downstream can be seen the small islands in the river marking the shallows at Boteler's Ford. From this vantage point Lee's Chief of Artillery, William N. Pendleton, dueled with Alfred Pleasonton's horse artillery on the 19th, and A. P. Hill battled troops of Fitz John Porter's V Corps on the 20th, both as rear guard actions.

ELMWOOD CEMETERY—*W. Va. Rt. 480, south of Shepherdstown on the left side of the road.*

Buried here are some 600 Confederates, most of whom were casualties of Antietam (or, the Battle of Sharpsburg, as the Confederates called it). One monument, erected by the Henry Kyd Douglas Camp of the Sons of Confederate Veterans in 1937, honors the men of Shepherdstown and Jefferson County who served the Confederacy. The county raised two companies of infantry for the Stonewall Brigade and two of cavalry for the Laurel Brigade. Another monument, erected June 6, 1870, memorializes unknown Confederate dead. Buried at Elmwood is Colonel Henry Kyd Douglas, who died in 1903.

TRAVEL AND ACCOMMODATIONS

Restaurants are scarce in the village of Sharpsburg. Accommodations and restaurants are more plentiful in Hagerstown, Frederick, and Shepherdstown, and a visit to Harper's Ferry is a must for the historical traveler. There are several excellent bed and breakfasts on or near the Antietam Battlefield, including:

• Historic Piper Farm House, Box 100, Sharpsburg, MD 21782; 301-797-1862. The Henry Piper farm, near Bloody Lane, was General James Longstreet's headquarters.

• Antietam Overlook Farm, Box 30, Keedysville, MD 21756; 800-878-4241. Keedysville is just east of the battlefield on Maryland Rt. 34.

• Inn at Antietam, 220 E. Main St., Sharpsburg, MD 21782; 301-432-6601. Located near the National Cemetery.

The principal interstate highway access to the Antietam Battlefield is I-70; the National Road (U.S. 40) parallels I-70 in the area. Nearby north-south access to I-70 and U.S. 40 is provided by I-81. Washington, DC, is 50 miles away. For further information contact the Antietam National Battlefield Park, Box 158, Sharpsburg, MD 21782; 301-432-5124. The Visitor Center has a regularly updated list of accommodations, restaurants, etc., and other travel-related literature.

BIBLIOGRAPHICAL NOTE and PHOTO CREDITS

SOURCES: Catton, Bruce, *Mr. Lincoln's Army*; Cunningham, D. and Miller, W. W. "Report of The Ohio Antietam Battlefield Commission"; Douglas, Henry Kyd, *I Rode With Stonewall*; Frassanito, William A., *Antietam: The Photographic Legacy of America's Bloodiest Day*; Freeman, Douglas Southall, *Lee's Lieutenants* vol. II; Murfin, James V., *The Gleam of Bayonets: The Battle of Antietam and the Maryland Campaign of 1862*; Robertson, James I., *The Stonewall Brigade*; Schildt, John W., *Drums Along the Antietam*; Sears, Stephen W., *Landscape Turned Red: The Battle of Antietam*; Warner, Ezra J., *Generals in Blue* and *Generals in Gray*; Williams, Alpheus S., *From the Cannon's Mouth: The Civil War Letters of General Alpheus S. Williams*; *Battles and Leaders of the Civil War*; *Official Records of the Union and Confederate Armies*; and numerous sources in the files of Antietam National Battlefield Park.

PHOTOGRAPHS are courtesy of: Library of Congress (LoC); National Archives (NA); USAMHI, Carlisle Barracks, PA; Valentine Museum (VM); Antietam National Battlefield, Sharpsburg, MD; Parks and History Association, Sharpsburg, MD; and Ben Ritter, Winchester, VA. Modern photographs are by David E. Roth (DER) of *Blue & Gray*. Cover Photo: Dunker Church (DER); Pg. 1: Dunker Church, wartime (LoC); Pg. 13: Robert E. Lee (LoC), James Longstreet (NA), Stonewall Jackson (NA); Pg. 37: George B. McClellan (NA), Fitz John Porter (USAMHI), Edwin V. Sumner (LoC), William B. Franklin (LoC); Pg. 43: Confederate dead along Hagerstown Pike (LoC); Pg. 50: Dunker Church (DER); Pg. 60: Miller's Cornfield (DER); Pg. 60: Joseph Hooker (LoC), John Bell Hood (VM); Pg. 68: Bloody Lane (DER); D. H. Hill (VM); Israel Richardson (LoC); Pg. 70: Confederate dead in Bloody Lane (LoC), George B. Anderson (LoC); Pg. 74: Burnside Bridge (DER), Ambrose E. Burnside (LoC); Pg. 80: Snavely's Ford (DER); Pg. 119: Lincoln and McClellan at Antietam (LoC); Pg. 120: A. P. Hill (VM); Pg. 121: Lincoln at the S. P. Grove house (LoC); Pg. 124: Philip Pry house (DER); Pg. 128: Pry's Mill (DER); Pg. 131: Clara Barton (LoC), Clara Barton Memorial (DER), Joseph K. F. Mansfield (USAMHI), Mansfield Monument (DER); Pg. 137: Robert E. Lee's headquarters (DER); Pg. 140: Ferry Hill Place (DER), Henry Kyd Douglas (Ben Ritter); Pg. 144: Boteler's Ford (DER); Pg. 148: Antietam National Cemetery (DER).

ACKNOWLEDGED for valuable cooperation and assistance are: Ted Alexander, Paul Chiles and Betty Otto of the National Park Service; the late James V. Murfin, and Stephen W. Sears, both excellent historians and authorities on the Maryland Campaign and Battle of Antietam; Tour Assistants were Jason Roth and William D. Holschuh.

APPENDIX 1

Order of Battle

Abbreviations: GEN, General; MG, Major General; BG, Brigadier General; COL, Colonel; LCOL, Lt. Colonel; MAJ, Major; CPT, Captain. (k) killed, (w) wounded, (mw) mortally wounded.

ARMY OF THE POTOMAC
MG George B. McClellan

I CORPS
MG Joseph Hooker (w)
BG George G. Meade

First Division:
BG Abner Doubleday

First Brigade:
COL Walter Phelps, Jr.
22nd New York
24th New York
30th New York
84th New York
2nd United States
Sharpshooters

Second Brigade:
LCOL J. William Hofmann
7th Indiana
76th New York
95th New York
56th Pennsylvania

Third Brigade:
BG Marsena R. Patrick
21st New York
23rd New York
35th New York
80th New York

Fourth Brigade:
BG John Gibbon
19th Indiana
2nd Wisconsin
6th Wisconsin
7th Wisconsin

Artillery:
CPT J. Albert Monroe
New Hampshire Light, 1st
Battery
1st New York Light, Battery L
1st Rhode Island Light,
Battery D
4th United States, Battery B

Second Division:
BG James B. Ricketts

First Brigade:
BG Abram Duryea
97th New York
104th New York
105th New York
107th Pennsylvania

Second Brigade:
COL William A. Christian

COL Peter Lyle
26th New York
94th New York
88th Pennsylvania
90th Pennsylvania

Third Brigade:
BG George L. Hartsuff (w)
COL Richard Coulter
12th Massachusetts
13th Massachusetts
83rd New York
11th Pennsylvania

Artillery:
1st Pennsylvania Light,
Battery F
Pennsylvania Light, Battery C

Third Division:
BG George G. Meade
BG Truman Seymour

First Brigade:
BG Truman Seymour
COL R. Biddle Roberts
1st Pennsylvania
2nd Pennsylvania
5th Pennsylvania
6th Pennsylvania
13th Pennsylvania

Second Brigade:
COL Albert L. Magilton
3rd Pennsylvania
4th Pennsylvania
7th Pennsylvania
8th Pennsylvania

Third Brigade:
LCOL Robert Anderson
9th Pennsylvania
10th Pennsylvania
11th Pennsylvania
12th Pennsylvania

Artillery:
1st Pennsylvania Light,
Battery A
1st Pennsylvania Light,
Battery B
5th United States, Battery C

II CORPS
MG Edwin V. Sumner

First Division:
MG Israel B. Richardson (mw)
BG John C. Caldwell
BG Winfield Scott Hancock

First Brigade:
BG John C. Caldwell
5th New Hampshire
7th New York
61st New York
64th New York
81st Pennsylvania

Second Brigade:
BG Thomas F. Meagher
COL John Burke
63rd New York
69th New York
88th New York
29th Massachusetts

Third Brigade:
COL John R. Brooke
2nd Delaware
52nd New York
57th New York
66th New York
53rd Pennsylvania

Artillery:
1st New York Light, Battery B
4th United States, Battery A
4th United States, Battery C

Second Division:
MG John Sedgwick (w)
BG Oliver O. Howard

First Brigade:
BG Willis A. Gorman
15th Massachusetts (1st Co.
Massachusetts Sharpshooters,
attached)
1st Minnesota (2nd Co.
Minnesota Sharpshooters,
attached)
34th New York
82nd New York

Second Brigade:
BG Oliver O. Howard
COL Joshua T. Owen
COL De Witte C. Baxter
69th Pennsylvania
71st Pennsylvania
72nd Pennsylvania
106th Pennsylvania

Third Brigade:
BG Napoleon J.T. Dana (w)
COL Norman J. Hall
19th Massachusetts
20th Massachusetts
7th Michigan
42nd New York
59th New York

Artillery:
1st Rhode Island Light,
Battery A
1st United States, Battery I

Third Division:
BG William H. French

First Brigade:
BG Nathan Kimball
14th Indiana
8th Ohio
132nd Pennsylvania
7th West Virginia

Second Brigade:
COL Dwight Morris
14th Connecticut
108th New York
130th Pennsylvania

Third Brigade:
BG Max Weber (w)
COL John W. Andrews
1st Delaware
5th Maryland
4th New York

Unattached Artillery:
1st New York Light, Battery G
1st Rhode Island Light,
Battery B
Battery G

IV Corps

First Division:
MG Darius N. Couch
(Attached to VI Corps)

First Brigade:
BG Charles Devens, Jr.
7th Massachusetts
10th Massachusetts
36th New York
2nd Rhode Island

Second Brigade:
BG Albion P. Howe
62nd New York
93rd Pennsylvania
98th Pennsylvania
102nd Pennsylvania
139th Pennsylvania

Third Brigade:
BG John Cochrane
65th New York
67th New York
122nd New York
23rd Pennsylvania
61st Pennsylvania
82nd Pennsylvania

Artillery:
1st Penna. Light, Battery C
1st Penna. Light, Battery D
New York Light, 3rd Battery
2nd United States, Battery G

V CORPS
MG Fitz John Porter

First Division:
MG George W. Morell

First Brigade:
COL James Barnes
2nd Maine
18th Massachusetts
1st Michigan
13th New York
25th New York
118th Pennsylvania
22nd Massachusetts (2nd Co.
Massachusetts Sharpshooters,
attached)

Second Brigade:
BG Charles Griffin
2nd District of Columbia
9th Massachusetts
32nd Massachusetts
4th Michigan
14th New York
62nd Pennsylvania

Third Brigade:
COL T.B.W. Stockton
16th Michigan (Brady's Co.,
Michigan Sharpshooters,
attached)
20th Maine
12th New York
17th New York
44th New York
83rd Pennsylvania

Sharpshooters:
1st United States

Artillery:
Massachusetts Light, Battery C
1st Rhode Island Light,
Battery C
5th United States, Battery D

Second Division:
BG George Sykes

First Brigade:
Lt. COL Robert C. Buchanan
3rd United States
4th United States
12th United States, 1st
Battalion
12th United States, 2nd
Battalion
14th United States, 1st
Battalion
14th United States, 2nd
Battalion

Second Brigade:
MAJ Charles S. Lovell
1st United States
2nd United States
6th United States
10th United States
11th United States

17th United States

Third Brigade:
COL Gouverneur K. Warren
5th New York
10th New York

Artillery:
1st United States, Battery E
1st United States, Battery G
5th United States, Battery I
5th United States, Battery K

Third Division:
BG Andrew A. Humphreys

First Brigade:
BG Erastus B. Tyler
91st Pennsylvania
126th Pennsylvania
129th Pennsylvania
134th Pennsylvania

Second Brigade:
COL Peter H. Allabach
123rd Pennsylvania
131st Pennsylvania
133rd Pennsylvania
155th Pennsylvania

Artillery:
CPT Lucius N. Robinson
1st New York Light, Battery C
1st Ohio Light, Battery L

Artillery Reserve:
LCOL William Hays
1st Battalion, New York Light,
Batteries A, B, C, D
New York Light, 5th Battery
1st United States, Battery K
4th United States, Battery G

VI CORPS
MG William B. Franklin

First Division:
MG Henry W. Slocum

First Brigade:
COL Alfred T.A. Torbert
1st New Jersey
2nd New Jersey
3rd New Jersey
4th New Jersey

Second Brigade:
COL Joseph J. Bartlett
5th Maine
16th Maine
27th New York
96th Pennsylvania

Third Brigade:
BG John Newton
18th New York
31st New York
32nd New York
95th Pennsylvania

Artillery:
CPT Emory Upton
Maryland Light, Battery A
Massachusetts Light, Battery A
New Jersey Light, Battery A
2nd United States, Battery D

Second Division:
MG William F. Smith

First Brigade:
BG Winfield S. Hancock
COL Amasa Cobb
6th Maine
43rd New York
49th Pennsylvania
137th Pennsylvania
5th Wisconsin

Second Brigade:
BG W.T.H. Brooks
2nd Vermont
3rd Vermont
4th Vermont
5th Vermont
6th Vermont

Third Brigade:
COL William H. Irwin
7th Maine
20th New York
33rd New York
49th New York
77th New York

Artillery:
CPT Romeyn B. Ayres
Maryland Light, Battery B
New York Light, 1st Battery
5th United States, Battery F

IX CORPS
MG Ambrose E. Burnside
BG Jacob D. Cox

First Division:
BG Orlando B. Willcox

First Brigade:
COL Benjamin C. Christ
28th Massachusetts
17th Michigan
79th New York
50th Pennsylvania

Second Brigade:
COL Thomas Welsh
8th Michigan
46th New York
45th Pennsylvania
100th Pennsylvania

Artillery:
Massachusetts Light,
8th Battery
2nd United States, Battery E

Second Division:
BG Samuel D. Sturgis

First Brigade:
BG James Nagle
2nd Maryland
6th New Hampshire
9th New Hampshire
48th Pennsylvania

Second Brigade:
BG Edward Ferrero
21st Massachusetts
35th Massachusetts
51st New York
51st Pennsylvania

Artillery:
Pennsylvania Light, Battery D
4th United States, Battery E

Third Division:
BG Isaac P. Rodman (mw)
COL Edward Harland

First Brigade:
COL Harrison S. Fairchild
9th New York
89th New York
103rd New York

Second Brigade:
COL Edward Harland
8th Connecticut
11th Connecticut
16th Connecticut
4th Rhode Island

Artillery:
5th United States, Battery A

Kanawha Division:
COL Eliakim P. Scammon

First Brigade:
COL Hugh Ewing
12th Ohio
23rd Ohio
30th Ohio

Artillery:
Ohio Light, 1st Battery

Cavalry:
Gilmore's and Harrison's Co's.,
West Virginia Cav.

Second Brigade:
COL George Crook
11th Ohio
28th Ohio
36th Ohio

Artillery:
Kentucky Light, Simmonds'
Battery

Cavalry:
Schambeck's Co., Chicago
Dragoons

Unattached Artillery:
2nd New York, Battery L

3rd United States, Battery L
3rd United States, Battery M

Unattached Cavalry:
6th New York (8 co's.)
Ohio Cavalry, 3rd Independent
Company

XII CORPS
MG Joseph K. F. Mansfield (mw)
BG Alpheus S. Williams

First Division:
BG Alpheus S. Williams
BG Samuel W. Crawford (w)
BG George H. Gordon

First Brigade:
BG Samuel W. Crawford
COL Joseph F. Knipe
10th Maine
28th New York
46th Pennsylvania
124th Pennsylvania
125th Pennsylvania
128th Pennsylvania

Third Brigade:
BG George H. Gordon
COL Thomas H. Ruger
27th Indiana
13th New Jersey
107th New York
3rd Wisconsin
2nd Massachusetts (Zouaves
d'Afrique, attached)

Second Division:
BG George S. Greene

First Brigade:
LCOL Hector Tyndale (w)
MAJ Orrin J. Crane
5th Ohio
7th Ohio
66th Ohio
28th Pennsylvania

Second Brigade:
COL Henry J. Stainrock
3rd Maryland
102nd New York
111th Pennsylvania

Third Brigade:
COL William B. Goodrich (k)
LCOL Jonathan Austin
3rd Delaware
60th New York
78th New York
Purnell (Maryland) Legion

Corps Artillery:
CPT Clermont L. Best
Maine Light, 4th Battery
Maine Light, 6th Battery
1st New York Light, Battery M
New York Light, 10th Battery
Pennsylvania Light, Battery E

Pennsylvania Light, Battery F
4th United States, Battery F

CAVALRY DIVISION
BG Alfred Pleasonton

First Brigade:
MAJ Charles J. Whiting
5th United States
6th United States

Second Brigade:
COL John F. Farnsworth
8th Illinois
3rd Indiana
1st Massachusetts
8th Pennsylvania

Third Brigade:
COL Richard H. Rush
4th Pennsylvania
6th Pennsylvania

Fourth Brigade:
COL Andrew T. McReynolds
1st New York
12th Pennsylvania

Fifth Brigade:
COL Benjamin F. Davis
8th New York
3rd Pennsylvania

Unattached:
15th Pennsylvania (detach.)

Artillery:
2nd United States, Battery A
2nd United States, Battery B
2nd United States, Battery L
2nd United States, Battery M
3rd United States, Battery C
3rd United States, Battery G

**ARMY OF
NORTHERN VIRGINIA**
GEN Robert E. Lee

LONGSTREET'S CORPS
MG James Longstreet

McLaws' Division:
MG Lafayette McLaws

Kershaw's Brigade:
BG Joseph B. Kershaw
2nd South Carolina
3rd South Carolina
7th South Carolina
8th South Carolina

Cobb's Brigade:
LCOL C.C. Sanders
LCOL William MacRae
16th Georgia
24th Georgia

15th North Carolina
Cobb's (Georgia) Legion (1/2)

Semmes' Brigade:
BG Paul J. Semmes
10th Georgia
53rd Georgia
15th Virginia
32nd Virginia

Barkdale's Brigade:
BG William Barksdale
13th Mississippi
17th Mississippi
18th Mississippi
21st Mississippi

Artillery:
COL Henry C. Cabell
Manly's (No. Carolina) Battery
Pulaski (Georgia) Artillery
Richmond (Fayette) Artillery
Richmond Howitzers, 1st Co.
Troup (Georgia) Artillery

Anderson's Division:
MG Richard H. Anderson (w)
BG Roger A. Pryor

Wilcox's Brigade:
COL Alfred Cumming
MAJ H.A. Herbert
8th Alabama
9th Alabama
10th Alabama
11th Alabama

Featherston's Brigade:
COL Carnot Posey
12th Mississippi
16th Mississippi
19th Mississippi
2nd Mississippi Battalion

Armistead's Brigade:
BG Lewis A. Armistead (w)
COL J. G. Hodges
9th Virginia
14th Virginia
38th Virginia
53rd Virginia
57th Virginia

Pryor's Brigade:
BG Roger A. Pryor
COL John C. Hately (w)
14th Alabama
2nd Florida
5th Florida
8th Florida
3rd Virginia

Mahone's Brigade (attached to
Pryor's Brigade):
COL William A. Parham
6th Virginia
12th Virginia
16th Virginia
41st Virginia
61st Virginia

Wright's Brigade:
BG Ambrose R. Wright (w)
COL Robert Jones (w)
COL William Gibson
44th Alabama
3rd Georgia
22nd Georgia
48th Georgia

Artillery:
CPT Cary F. Grimes (k)
MAJ John S. Saunders
Donaldsonville (Louisiana)
Artillery (Maurin's Battery)
Huger's (Norfolk) Battery
Moorman's (Lynchburg)
Battery
Grimes' (Portsmouth) Battery

Jones' Division:
BG David R. Jones

Toombs' Brigade:
BG Robert Toombs
COL Henry L. Benning
2nd Georgia
15th Georgia
17th Georgia
20th Georgia

Drayton's Brigade:
BG Thomas F. Drayton
50th Georgia
51st Georgia
15th South Carolina
3rd South Carolina Battalion

Pickett's Brigade:
BG Richard B. Garnett
8th Virginia
18th Virginia
19th Virginia
28th Virginia
56th Virginia

Kemper's Brigade:
BG James L. Kemper
1st Virginia
7th Virginia
11th Virginia
17th Virginia
24th Virginia

Jenkins' Brigade:
COL Joseph Walker
1st South Carolina (Volunteers)
2nd South Carolina Rifles
5th South Carolina
6th South Carolina
4th South Carolina Battalion
Palmetto (South Carolina)
Sharpshooters

Anderson's Brigade:
COL George T. Anderson
1st Georgia
7th Georgia
8th Georgia
9th Georgia
11th Georgia

Artillery:
Wise (Virginia) Artillery (J.S. Brown's Battery)

Walker's Division:
BG John G. Walker

Walker's Brigade:
COL Van H. Manning (w)
COL E.D. Hall
3rd Arkansas
27th North Carolina
46th North Carolina
48th North Carolina
30th Virginia

Artillery:
French's (Stafford) Battery

Ransom's Brigade:
BG Robert Ransom, Jr.
24th North Carolina
25th North Carolina
35th North Carolina
49th North Carolina

Artillery:
Branch's (Petersburg) Field Artillery

Hood's Division:
BG John Bell Hood

Hood's Brigade:
COL William T. Wofford
18th Georgia
1st Texas
4th Texas
5th Texas
Hampton (South Carolina) Legion

Law's Brigade:
COL Evander M. Law
4th Alabama
2nd Mississippi
11th Mississippi
6th North Carolina

Artillery:
MAJ B.W. Frobel
German (Charleston) Artillery
Palmetto (South Carolina) Artillery
Rowan (North Carolina) Artillery

Evans' (Independent) Brigade:
BG Nathan G. Evans
COL P.F. Stevens
17th South Carolina
18th South Carolina
22nd South Carolina
23rd South Carolina
Holcombe (South Carolina) Legion

Artillery:
Macbeth (South Carolina) Artillery

Corps Artillery:

1st Battalion:
COL John B. Walton
Washington (Louisiana) Artillery, 1st, 2nd, 3rd, 4th Cos.

2nd Battalion:
COL Stephen D. Lee
Ashland (Virginia) Artillery
Bedford (Virginia) Artillery
Brooks (South Carolina) Artillery
Eubank's (Bath) Battery
Madison (Louisiana) Light Artillery
Parker's (Richmond) Battery

JACKSON'S CORPS
MG Thomas J. "Stonewall" Jackson

Ewell's Division:
BG Alexander R. Lawton (w)
BG Jubal A. Early

Lawton's Brigade:
COL Marcellus Douglas (k)
MAJ J.H. Lowe
13th Georgia
26th Georgia
31st Georgia
38th Georgia
60th Georgia
61st Georgia

Early's Brigade:
BG Jubal A. Early
COL William Smith (w)
13th Virginia
25th Virginia
31st Virginia
44th Virginia
49th Virginia
52nd Virginia
58th Virginia

Trimble's Brigade:
COL James A. Walker (w)
15th Alabama
12th Georgia
21st Georgia
21st North Carolina
1st North Carolina Battalion

Hays' Brigade:
BG Harry T. Hays
5th Louisiana
6th Louisiana
7th Louisiana
8th Louisiana
14th Louisiana

Artillery:
MAJ A.R. Courtney
Louisiana Guard Artillery (D'Aquin's Battery)
Staunton (Virginia) Artillery (Balthis' Battery)
Johnson's (Virginia) Battery

Hill's Light Division:
MG A.P. Hill

Branch's Brigade:
BG Lawrence O'B. Branch (k)
COL Thomas H. Lane
7th North Carolina
18th North Carolina
28th North Carolina
33rd North Carolina
37th North Carolina

Gregg's Brigade:
BG Maxcy Gregg
1st South Carolina (Provisional)
1st South Carolina Rifles
12th South Carolina
13th South Carolina
14th South Carolina

Field's Brigade:
COL John M. Brockenbrough
40th Virginia
47th Virginia
55th Virginia
22nd Virginia Battalion

Archer's Brigade:
BG James J. Archer
COL Peter Turney
19th Georgia
1st Tennessee (Provisional)
7th Tennessee
14th Tennessee

Pender's Brigade:
BG William D. Pender
COL R.H. Brewer
16th North Carolina
22nd North Carolina
34th North Carolina
38th North Carolina

Artillery:
LCOL R.L. Walker
Fredericksburg (Virginia) Artillery (Braxton's Battery)
Pee Dee (South Carolina) Artillery (McIntosh's Battery)
Purcell (Richmond) Artillery (Pegram's Battery)
Crenshaw's (Richmond) Battery

Jackson's Division:
BG John R. Jones (w)
BG William E. Starke (k)
COL Andrew J. Grigsby

Winder's Brigade:
COL Andrew J. Grigsby
LCOL R.D. Gardner (w)
MAJ H.J. Williams
4th Virginia
5th Virginia
27th Virginia
33rd Virginia

Taliaferro's Brigade:
COL James W. Jackson (w)

COL James L. Sheffield
47th Alabama
48th Alabama
23rd Virginia
37th Virginia

Jones' Brigade:
CPT John E. Penn (w)
CPT A.C. Page (w)
CPT R.W. Withers
21st Virginia
42nd Virginia
48th Virginia
1st Virginia Battalion

Starke's Brigade:
BG William E. Starke (k)
COL Leroy A. Stafford (w)
COL Edmund Pendleton
1st Louisiana
2nd Louisiana
9th Louisiana
10th Louisiana
15th Louisiana
1st Louisiana Battalion

Artillery:
MAJ L. M. Schumaker
Alleghany (Virginia) Artillery
(Carpenter's Battery)
Danville (Virginia) Artillery
(Wooding's Battery)
Lee (Virginia) Battery (Raine's
Battery)
Rockbridge (Virginia) Artillery
(Poague's Battery)
Brockenbrough's (Maryland)
Battery

Hill's Division:
MG D.H. Hill

Ripley's Brigade:
BG Roswell S. Ripley (w)
COL George Doles
4th Georgia
44th Georgia
1st North Carolina
3rd North Carolina

Rodes' Brigade:
BG Robert E. Rodes
3rd Alabama
5th Alabama
6th Alabama
12th Alabama
26th Alabama

Garland's Brigade:
COL D.K. McRae
5th North Carolina
12th North Carolina
13th North Carolina
20th North Carolina
23rd North Carolina

Anderson's Brigade:
BG George B. Anderson (mw)
COL C.C. Tew (k)
COL R.T. Bennett
2nd North Carolina
4th North Carolina
14th North Carolina
30th North Carolina

Colquitt's Brigade:
BG Alfred H. Colquitt
13th Alabama
6th Georgia
23rd Georgia
27th Georgia
28th Georgia

Artillery:
MAJ C.F. Pierson
Jones' (Virginia) Battery
King William (Virginia)
Artillery
Hardaway's (Alabama) Battery
Jeff Davis (Alabama) Artillery

RESERVE ARTILLERY
BG William N. Pendleton

Cutts' Battalion:
LCOL A.S. Cutts
Blackshears' (Georgia) Battery
Patterson's (Georgia) Battery

Irwin (Georgia) Artillery (Lame's
Battery)
Ross' (Georgia) Battery
Lloyd's (North Carolina) Battery

Jones' Battalion:
MAJ H. P. Jones
Turner's (Virginia) Battery
Orange (Virginia) Artillery
(Peyton's Battery)
Morris (Virginia) Artillery (Page's
Battery)
Wimbish's (Virginia) Battery

Unattached:
Magruder Artillery, Cutshaw's
(Virginia) Battery

CAVALRY DIVISION
MG James Ewell Brown
"Jeb" Stuart

Hampton's Brigade:
BG Wade Hampton
1st North Carolina
2nd South Carolina
Cobb's (Georgia) Legion (1/2)
Jeff Davis (Mississippi) Legion

Lee's Brigade:
BG Fitzhugh Lee
1st Virginia
3rd Virginia
4th Virginia
5th Virginia
9th Virginia

Robertson's Brigade:
COL Thomas T. Munford
2nd Virginia
7th Virginia
12th Virginia

Horse Artillery:
MAJ John Pelham
Pelham's (Virginia) Battery
Chew's (Virginia) Battery
Hart's (South Carolina) Battery

APPENDIX 2

Strengths and Losses at Antietam

Losses in Civil War battles are always difficult to ascertain. The Confederates, in particular, seemed to lack the bookkeeping discipline of their Union counterparts in recording such statistics. In some instances, commanders included South Mountain losses with Antietam losses in their reports.

James Murfin in *The Gleam of Bayonets* mentions 12,410 Federal and 10,291 Confederate losses as a good estimate, though he states that Confederate casualties range in estimates from 8,000 to 13,724. His introduction in Part I of the Antietam Tour mentions 24,000 combined casualties. Stephen W. Sears in *Landscape Turned Red* states 12,401 Federal and 10,318 Confederate losses, tempering the statement with caution that Confederate losses have "never been precisely reckoned." Thomas Livermore in *Numbers and Losses in the Civil War in America 1861-1865* places the figures at 12,410 Federal and 13,724 Confederate losses. Though 24,000 is the generally accepted figure, estimates of total losses (Federal and Confederate) ranging from 22,000 to 26,000 should be considered "reasonable" counts, none of which would rob Antietam of its distinction as the single bloodiest day of the Civil War.

Other "number debates" surrond the total numbers present at Antietam. Estimates range from 70,000 to 95,000 Federals, usually distinguishing between "full roster" and "effectives," and 30,000 to 55,000 Confederates (disregarding the exaggerated estimates of certain Federal officers). Reasonable estimates of the opposing "effective" strengths at Antietam are 70,000 Federals and 35,000 Confederates.

Index

Other titles by Blue & Gray Magazine and its book publishing division, The General's Books:

The Story of Camp Chase
by William H. Knauss

Yankee Quaker Confederate General: The Curious Career of Bushrod Rust Johnson
by Charles M. Cummings

Embrace An Angry Wind: The Confederacy's Last Hurrah—
Spring Hill, Franklin and Nashville
by Wiley Sword

The 15th Ohio Volunteers and Its Campaigns, 1861-1865
by Capt. Alexis Cope

Blue & Gray Magazine is published bi-monthly. The General's Books regularly issues a catalog containing more than 1,000 Civil War titles from a hundred different publishers. For more information call: 1-800-CIVIL WAR (or 1-800-248-4592) or write Blue & Gray, 522 Norton Road, Columbus, OH 43228.